D1570999

STRINGBAGS
in
ACTION

STRINGBAGS
in
ACTION

—ᴧᴧᴧ—

The Attack on Taranto 1940
&
The Loss of the *Bismarck* 1941

VICE ADMIRAL B.B. SCHOFIELD,
CB CBE

Pen & Sword
MARITIME

The Attack on Taranto
First published in Great Britain in 1973

The Loss of the Bismarck
First published in Great Britain in 1972

Reprinted in this format in 2011
By Pen and Sword Maritime
an imprint of
Pen and Sword Books Ltd
47 Church Street
Barnsley
South Yorkshire S70 2AS

ISBN 978 1 84884 388 2

A CIP record for this book is available from the British Library

Printed and bound in England
by the MPG Books Group

Typeset by Chic Media

Pen and Sword Books Ltd incorporates the imprints of
Pen and Sword Aviation, Pen and Sword Maritime, Pen and Sword Military,
Wharncliffe Local History, Pen and Sword Select,
Pen and Sword Military Classics and Leo Cooper.

For a complete list of Pen and Sword titles please contact
Pen and Sword Books Limited
47 Church Street, Barnsley, South Yorkshire, S70 2AS, England
E-mail: enquiries@pen-and-sword.co.uk
Website: www.pen-and-sword.co.uk

Contents

—ɱ—

The Attack on Taranto 1940

The Loss of the Bismarck 1941

Foreword

My Stringbag flies over the ocean,
My Stringbag flies over the sea.
If it weren't for King George's Swordfish,
Where the hell would the Royal Navy be?

The popular lyric sung by Fleet Air Arm pilots to the tune of 'My Bonnie Lies over the Ocean' during the Second World War makes a valid point. Without the legendary Swordfish plane, the Royal Navy would not have retained its mastery of the seas. Threatened by the Italian Navy in the Mediterranean and German submarines in the Atlantic, if Britain was to prevail in the inevitable naval battles to come, it was essential to have the ability for aerial attack.

'Stringbags in Action' tells the story of two major events in 1940 and 1941 – the attack on Taranto and the sinking of the *Bismarck* - in which the Swordfish played a significant role. With a cruising speed of less than 100 mph, the slow-moving bi-plane had been built in the 1930s by Fairey Aviation Company. Designed to spot the fall of a warship's gunfire, with a torpedo strapped under the fuselage, the plane was effective both in naval reconnaissance and as an aerial torpedo bomber. Officially called the Fairey Torpedo-Spotter Reconnaissance, with space-saving folding wings, it was given the name Swordfish; the bracing wires between the wings, and its ability to carry an assortment of pieces of equipment - like a housewife's shopping bag - also meant that the Swordfish was affectionately called a 'Stringbag' by the brave young men who flew in it. Against its deficiencies, it surpassed the speedier monoplanes by being easy to handle and was relatively resistant, both against attack and in seaborne sorties in adverse weather conditions. 'Although obsolescent when the war began,' writes my father, B.B. Schofield, 'the Swordfish remained operational throughout the war and proved its value in anti-submarine warfare many times over.'

After Italy's entry into the war in June 1940, Swordfish planes, based in Malta, started to attack Italian shipping in the Mediterranean, sinking on average 50,000 tons of shipping per month. Then came the ambitious plan to attack the Italian fleet based in southern Italy in the harbour of Taranto. Twenty-one Swordfish planes were used 'on which,' my father writes, 'the success or failure of the operation depended.' The following year, the German battleship, *Bismarck*, embarked on her first and only mission, leaving the safe haven of the Baltic Sea with the heavy cruiser *Prinz Eugen*. With a speed surpassing any of the British battleships, the *Bismarck* posed the greatest threat yet to Britain's merchant shipping. Once intelligence reports were received that she was heading for the Atlantic, the British Home Fleet seized the opportunity to deploy a large force, involving Royal Navy battleships, destroyers, cruisers and aircraft carriers, to attack her. After the disastrous sinking of HMS *Hood*, the pursuit of the *Bismarck* became an epic battle to find and destroy her, before she could reach safety in the French port of Brest. Yet again, the Stringbags were in action.

Victoria Schofield, 2010.

The Attack on Taranto
1940

Introduction

It is not really surprising that there was a great deal of opposition to the introduction of aircraft into the Royal Navy. The Service had only recently adjusted itself to the revolutionary change from sail to steam and, at first it appeared that here was yet another invention threatening to cause a new upheaval. So when, in March 1907, the Wright Brothers offered the Admiralty the opportunity of acquiring the patent rights of the flying machine in which, three years previously, they had made history by achieving the first sustained flight, it was politely declined. Almost alone amongst senior naval officers of that period, the First Sea Lord, Admiral Sir John (later Lord) Fisher realised the possibilities of this invention. A year later he sent an officer, Captain (later Admiral Sir) Reginald Bacon, to France to report on the first international air race which took place at Rheims. In that year Louis Bleriot flew across the Channel and Britain's insular security was breached. Fisher could see, in the ability to fly, a means of obtaining intelligence of the disposition of an enemy fleet both in harbour and at sea and it was natural that, at first, the lighter-than-air ship appeared more suited to this role than the heavier-than-air craft. The German Navy was of the same opinion and gave Count Zeppelin every encouragement with the development of the famous rigid airships named after him.

The first British naval airship was the 512ft (155½ m) long *Mayfly*. She took two years to build but she had a life of only four months, being caught by a gust of wind and destroyed as she emerged from her hangar on 29 September 1911. The disaster somewhat dampened the Navy's enthusiasm for aviation and it was due to two members of the newly formed Royal Aero Club, Francis McLean and C.B. Cockburn, who offered to lend the Admiralty aircraft and teach selected officers to fly, that the spark was rekindled. In response to a call for volunteers over 200 names were sent in, but only four were chosen, subsequently increased to five, and all gained the Royal Aero Club's Aviator's certificate within six weeks of commencing training. Meanwhile another officer, Commander Schwann, who had been connected with the building of the ill-fated *Mayfly*, had bought an aircraft with private funds which he had fitted with floats and with which it was demonstrated that an airplane could take off and land on the water. The enthusiasm of these early aviators soon led to flights being made from special platforms erected on warships and also to the construction of seaplanes. The Admiralty, now impressed by all these activities, was moved to set out the duties which they considered naval aircraft should be capable of performing. These were:

Reconnaissance of enemy ports;
Reconnaissance of the area surrounding a fleet at sea;
The location of submarines;
The detection of minefields;
Spotting the fall of shot for the guns of the fleet.

The year 1912 saw the beginning of the Naval Air Arm. In November of the previous year the Prime Minister, Mr Asquith, invited the Committee of Imperial Defence 'to consider the future of aerial navigation for both naval and military purposes; the means which might be taken to secure to this country an efficient air service; and also whether steps should be taken to co-ordinate the study of aviation in the Navy and the Army.' A technical sub-committee, appointed to consider the matter, recommended that a single service be formed to be known as The Royal Flying Corps, which would comprise two wings, one naval and one military, and the formation of an Air Committee of twelve members. A central pool of pilots was to be created, drawn from officers of both services, trained at a central school and available for duty with either of them. These recommendations were approved by Parliament on 11 May 1912.

The Admiralty at once objected to the interchangeability of pilots because of the very different conditions pertaining to operations over the sea and the land. Thanks to the eloquence of the First Lord, Mr Winston Churchill, the Cabinet was won over to the Admiralty's point of view and on 1 July 1914 the naval wing of the Royal Flying Corps formally assumed the name by which it had already become known - The Royal Naval Air Service - and became an adjunct to the Royal Navy. While these deliberations had been in progress, the naval aviators had been considering the problem of bombing ships and flying off them under way, and they had made considerable progress with both of them. Also, thanks to Mr Churchill's ready support, the new service was steadily expanding, so that when war broke out in 1914, the RNAS could boast of seven airships, 52 seaplanes and 39 aircraft with a personnel strength of approximately 138 officers and 600 men. As the Royal Flying Corps was now part of the Army and would therefore have to accompany it to France, the RNAS was made responsible for the defence of Great Britain from air attack, a task for which it was not really suited and which later was partly responsible for its undoing.

Meanwhile, the Admiralty had discovered that seaplanes lacked the range to carry out their primary duty of scouting ahead of the fleet and in consequence would have to be carried in ships to the scene of operations. This led to the conversion of the old cruiser, HMS *Hermes*, and certain selected merchant ships into seaplane carriers. They were equipped with facilities for servicing the seaplanes and for hoisting them in and out. From the start, the German Zeppelins were made a priority target by the Government because of their ability to drop bombs on Britain and also because they were used by the German Navy for reconnaissance of the North Sea. As a result, plans were worked out for attacking the Zeppelins from both sea and land in their sheds in various parts of Germany. In order to reach some of the more distant ones RNAS aircraft were sent to Belgium from whence, after two unsuccessful attacks, they succeeded in destroying one, the Z.9, at Dusseldorf. An attack on Cuxhaven, although doing little damage, induced part of the German fleet to move to the Baltic. All in all the first four months of war vindicated the faith of those who believed that aircraft would be able to make a useful contribution to the war at sea, despite the fact that the German fleet had been somewhat coy in showing itself.

The Admiralty, to which Fisher had now returned as First Sea Lord, had, under his dynamic direction, embarked on an extensive programme of expansion of the RNAS, especially since the U-boat menace was beginning to make itself increasingly felt. It appeared that one way to get on top of it was to bomb the submarines in their lairs, but it was not long before it was discovered that such a form of attack was singularly ineffective. As an alternative, some small non-rigid airships were built to patrol the waters around the British coast in which the U-boats were operating. These, at least, had the effect of making it more difficult for the U-boats to operate on the surface and sink ships by gunfire, and it also enabled their positions to be reported so that surface craft could be sent to hunt them.

The Zeppelin raids on Britain once again focused attention on the need to find ways and means of destroying them and the RNAS gained its first Victorian Cross through the action of Flight Sub Lieutenant Warneford. While flying a Morane aircraft he destroyed LZ.37 in the air over Belgium. However it was apparent that seaplanes were not as suitable as land planes for attacking airships since they did not have as good a rate of climb, the secret of success being the ability to rise above the airship and attack it from there. The Commander-in-Chief of the Grand Fleet, Admiral Sir John (later Admiral of the Fleet Viscount) Jellicoe, was also asking for aircraft fitted with radio to scout ahead of the fleet, but, as mentioned, the poor endurance of the seaplane was a handicap and the available seaplane carriers were not fast enough to keep up with the fleet. In an endeavour to comply with his request, the Admiralty acquired a former Cunard passenger ship, the *Campania*, and fitted her with facilities for operating seaplanes, but two more years were to elapse before the problem of operating wheel-fitted aircraft from ships was to be solved satisfactorily.

Abroad the RNAS was adding to its laurels in support of operations at the Dardanelles and history was made when, on 12 August 1915, Flight Commander C.H.K. Edmunds, in a Short seaplane with a 14in (356mm) torpedo slung under its fuselage, released it against a 5,000 ton Turkish supply ship lying off Injin Burnu. The ship listed and sank. The success was repeated in double measure five days later. On 19 November the service gained its second Victoria Cross when Squadron Commander R. Bell-Davies, flying a single-seater Nieuport aircraft, alighted in enemy territory and, under fire, successfully rescued the pilot of another aircraft which had been obliged to force land.

Another type of operation involving the use of aircraft took place off the coast of German East Africa where the cruiser *Königsberg*, after a brief cruise as a raider in the Indian Ocean, had taken refuge in the delta of the Rufigi River beyond the range of the guns of a watching British cruiser. She was ultimately destroyed by fire from shallow draft monitors assisted by spotting corrections passed from a Short seaplane brought from Bombay and flown by Flight Lieutenant J.T. Cull with Sub Lieutenant H.J. Arnold as his Observer.

The heterogeneous collection of aircraft, with which the RNAS was now equipped, was creating difficulties of maintenance and spare parts, and early in 1916, the Admiralty set about re-organizing the whole service. It was decided to concentrate on three main types of aircraft, viz. a large bomber with a range of 300 miles, able to carry a bomb load of 500lbs (227kg); a fast single-seater fighter with a high rate of climb and armed with a machine gun firing through the propeller; and a seaplane capable of carrying a torpedo. At the same time, attempts were to be made to design more powerful engines and better radio sets. Fortunately too, at this time, it was decided that the Royal Flying Corps should relieve the RNAS of responsibility for the air defence of Great Britain.

In March 1916, it was decided that an attempt should be made to discover and destroy the Zeppelin sheds thought to be located at Hoyer, a small town on the Schleswig-Holstein coast, opposite the island of Sylt. The seaplane carrier *Vindex* escorted by the Harwich Force of cruisers and destroyers was selected for the task and was supported by the battle-cruiser force. Although three out of five seaplanes which took part in the attack failed to return, and the Zeppelin sheds were further inland at Tondern, the raid caused the High Seas fleet to raise steam and almost precipitated the fleet action which took place two months later off the coast of Jutland. In this action, which occurred on 31 May, the Germans had planned to use their Zeppelins but were prevented from doing so by the unfavourable weather conditions. Both the British Grand and Battle-cruiser Fleets had seaplane carriers attached to them. Just before the action began, the *Engadine*, attached to the former, launched a seaplane which sighted and shadowed a part of the German battle-cruiser force before being obliged to force land with a broken petrol pipe. Running repairs were made and the seaplane took off again but, by now, action had been joined and no further thought was given to air reconnaissance, although an early report of the position of the German battle fleet could well have altered the whole course of events. Due to not receiving the signal to raise steam, the Grand Fleet's seaplane carrier, *Campania*, left harbour too late to take any part in the action. However, the flight of the *Engadine's* seaplane had demonstrated for the first time how valuable air reconnaissance could be in giving early information of the enemy's presence.

By the end of the year the RNAS had established itself as an integral part of the Royal Navy. This was recognised by the appointment on 31 January 1917 of an additional member of the Board of Admiralty, known as the Fifth Sea Lord, with responsibility for all matters affecting naval aviation. This was the year which saw the appearance of the aircraft carrier proper. She was a merchant ship being built in England for Italy called the *Conte Rosso*, and was fitted with a flush deck forward for launching wheel-fitted aircraft and one aft for operating seaplanes. She was renamed HMS *Argus* and was to provide long and useful service extending into the Second World War. At the same time the fast armourless battle–cruiser, HMS *Furious*, had her foremost single 18in (457mm) gun turret removed and a large flying deck with a hangar beneath built in its place. It was onboard this ship that, on 3 August 1917, Squadron Commander E.H. Dunning, DSC, made the first ever landing of a wheel-fitted aircraft on a ship at sea. His death after repeating the achievement two days later was a tragedy for the RNAS but his feat was an historic one. It led to the adoption of the through deck, enabling aircraft to take off over the bows and land on over the stern. However, the problem of bringing them to rest satisfactorily and without damaging the aircraft was not solved for several years.

The successful aircraft designer, T.M. Sopwith, had been invited to submit a plan for an aircraft capable of carrying an 18in (457mm) torpedo. In June 1917 he produced the Cuckoo, a single-seater wood and fabric aircraft powered by a 200 HP Sunbeam Arab engine and capable of a speed of 98mph. It was the first wheel-fitted aircraft to be so armed. On trials it proved highly successful, but the first operational squadron did not join the fleet until October 1918, and so it was never tried out in action.

The public outcry resulting from the raids carried out with apparent impunity on Britain by the Zeppelin airships coupled with the appearance on the western front in France of German aircraft superior to anything possessed by the Royal Flying Corps and squabbles between the Navy and Army for the supply of aircraft, produced a crisis which called for immediate Government intervention. A committee under the chairmanship of the Prime Minister, Lloyd George, was set up to look into the matter. As his deputy, the Prime Minister selected Field Marshal Jan Christian Smuts, a member of the War Cabinet, statesman, soldier, philosopher and lawyer, but without any special qualifications for the task. Lord Milner, always ready with advice, wrote to him accusing the soldiers and sailors at the War Office and Admiralty of not grasping the fact that they were faced with a new kind of warfare, and 'that, besides the help they have given the Army and Navy, the airmen will have to fight battles on their own.' This did not accord with Generalissimo Foch's view that the first duty of fighting aeroplanes was to assist the troops on the ground and that air fighting was not to be sought except as necessary for the fulfilment of this duty. The Committee, after only four weeks of deliberation, came out with a recommendation that the RNAS and the RFC should be amalgamated into one service to be known as the Royal Air Force under a separate Ministry. In addition, there was to be 'a small part specially trained for work with the Navy and a small part for work with the Army; these two small portions probably becoming, in the future, an arm of the older service'. Although the hope was thus held out of a restoration of a separate naval air arm at some time, it was not realised without a long and bitter struggle, which lasted almost twenty years, between the Admiralty and the new Air Ministry.

It was evident that carrier design was an important factor in the future progress of naval aviation. In 1917 the Admiralty had taken over the Chilean battleship *Almirante Cochrane* of 22,000 tons which was being built in Britain at Armstrong's shipyard on the Clyde. She was redesigned with an all-over flight deck and an island superstructure on the starboard side containing the bridge and wheel house – a complete innovation – which was to become standard practice in the majority of aircraft carriers. She was launched on 8 June 1918 and, like the *Argus*, was to give many years of service under the name of HMS *Eagle*, until lost during the Second World War. At the same time, a contract was awarded to Armstrong's for the design of a carrier to be built as such from the keel upwards. Christened HMS *Hermes* she was only half the size of the *Eagle*, but she too gave nearly twenty years of service. The *Eagle* was commissioned in 1922 and the *Hermes*, a year later.

It was not long before the Admiralty and the Air Ministry found themselves at loggerheads over the training of personnel, the former being dissatisfied with the quality of the pilots allocated for duty with the Navy. Then came the Washington Treaty for the limitation of armaments, signed in 1922, and two years later the Admiralty took stock of the situation regarding the number of carriers and aircraft needed and their tactical employment. The three carriers, *Furious*, *Eagle* and *Hermes*, (the *Argus* was not regarded as operational) totalled 55,900 tons and the Treaty allowed Britain and the United States a total carrier tonnage of 80,000. In addition, any country was allowed, if it wished, to build two carriers of not more than 33,000 tons each. This clause had been agreed to allow the United States to convert the two battle-cruiser hulls, *Lexington* and *Saratoga*, to carriers, and Britain made use of it to convert the two fast battle-cruisers, *Courageous* and *Glorious*, in a similar manner. However it was not until 1928 that these ships joined the fleet and Britain still had 24,000 tons available to complete her quota. Due to stringent economy in defence expenditure the gap was not filled until 1936 when construction was begun on a new carrier, HMS *Ark Royal*, which was commissioned in 1938.

With regard to the aircraft, in 1924 the Fairey Flycatcher entered service as the standard single-seater fighter and three years later the Fairey III F, a three-seater spotter reconnaissance aircraft, was introduced. The Admiralty, again contrary to the Air Ministry, considered the torpedo as the best weapon with which to arm ship-borne strike aircraft, but its employment demanded a special type of aircraft. Since the Ministry did not see eye to eye with the Admiralty (in their opinion the bomb was to be preferred), and it was responsible for the production of aircraft, it is not surprising that this requirement did not rank very high on its list of priorities. The Cuckoo's successor was the Blackburn Dart which entered service in 1923. It was a single-seater aircraft and suffered from the grave disadvantage that the pilot, besides flying the aircraft, had to work out the right firing angle and also operate the release mechanism. Next came the Blackburn Ripon which entered service in 1929. A two-seater, it was slightly faster and had a greater range that the Dart, although the rate of climb was not so good. The Ripon was succeeded by the Baffin and Shark, both of which offered only marginally better performance and their first line service was noticeably brief. In 1936 came the famous Fairey Swordfish, popularly known as the 'Stringbag'. Although its performance was very little better than that of the Ripon and was not so good as the Shark, its magnificent handling qualities endeared it to all who flew it and it earned the respect of thousands of Fleet Air Arm pilots.

Thus, on the outbreak of the Second World War in 1939, it was the standard Torpedo-Spotter-Reconnaissance (TSR) aircraft in the British fleet. Compared with contemporary torpedo-carrying aircraft, such as the Douglas TBD.1 Devastator of the US Navy, (which had a maximum speed of 200 knots and a range of 985 miles, armed with a 1,000lb torpedo) or the Naka BSN.2 (Kate) of the Japanese Navy (with a speed of 235 knots, a range of 1,400 miles, and a 1,764lb torpedo), the Swordfish, with a maximum speed of 125 knots, a range of 450 miles and a 1,200lb torpedo, was obsolescent. Even its successor, the Albacore, with a speed of 155 knots and a range of 630 miles, was no match for its foreign competitors so that in the final stages of the war the Royal Navy's carriers had to be equipped with American aircraft. As regards to the torpedoes themselves, little had been done in the inter-war years to improve these very effective weapons. However a new pistol was designed which functioned both on impact and, if set to run under a ship, also as a result of the vessel's inherent magnetism. This, as will be seen, was to play an important part in the story which follows.

In 1937 the Admiralty, thanks to the determination of the First Sea Lord, Admiral Sir Ernle (later Admiral of the Fleet Lord) Chatfield, regained administrative and operational control of the Fleet Air Arm. It had been a long, hard and, at times, embittered struggle and the victory was, in a sense, a Pyrrhic one since, with another major war just around the corner there was insufficient time to make good the deficiencies which had resulted from twenty years of divided control. Fortunately, when in 1936 Germany's aggressive posture persuaded the British Government to sanction a certain amount of rearmament expenditure, orders were given to lay down two carriers of the Illustrious class (see Appendix 7) and the following year two more were ordered. In each of the 1938 and 1939 Navy Estimates, provision was made for the construction of an improved Illustrious class carrier, with the result that on the outbreak of war in 1939 there were altogether six of the ships building, of which two had been launched, HMS *Illustrious*, on 5 April 1939 and HMS *Formidable* on 17 August, while a third ship, HMS *Victorious* took to the water on 14 September, ten days after war was declared.

When, in September 1938, Hitler invaded Czechoslovakia, an action which led to the mobilisation of the British fleet, that part of it which was stationed in the Mediterranean and based in Malta, moved to its war base at Alexandria, Egypt. There the Commander-in-Chief, Admiral Sir Dudley Pound, began preparations for attacking the Italian fleet, should Mussolini decide to rally to the support of his Axis partner in the event of war. At that time, the Mediterranean fleet included one aircraft carrier, HMS *Glorious*, which was equipped with one squadron of

Nimrod and Osprey fighters and three squadrons, each of twelve Swordfish TSR aircraft. Under her Commanding Officer, Captain Arthur Lumley St George Lyster, CVO, RN, these squadrons had been brought to a very high pitch of efficiency as a result of constant practice. Lyster, who features again in this story, was a gunnery specialist, but he appreciated that there was a great future for naval aircraft, an opinion reinforced by experience in his present command. A heavy jowled man with a sardonic sense of humour, he inspired confidence in his subordinates, whose problems he readily shared and understood. Yet he could be tough when the occasion demanded. Admiral Pound, who had arrived in 1935 to take over command of the Mediterranean at the time of the crisis caused by Mussolini's invasion of Abyssinia, recollected that, at that time, a plan had been worked out using Fleet Air Arm aircraft for an attack on the Italian fleet in its main base at Taranto. Captain Lyster had located a copy of this plan in his ship's secret files when he took over command, so he was not in the least surprised when Admiral Pound sent for him one day and told him to bring it up to date. After going over it with his Commander (Flying) and Senior Observer, he was able to report back to the Commander in Chief that, despite the growing strength of the Italian Air Force (Regia Aeronautica), he was confident that, if surprise could be achieved, the odds were in favour of dealing the enemy a crippling blow. After what has been said about the general attitude of senior naval officers to the Fleet Air Arm, that initiation of this plan is all the more remarkable. It shows that there were some forward thinking officers who visualised the potential striking power of aircraft and their ability to exploit the vulnerability of ships to attack by torpedo. As an American Admiral is credited with saying apropos of bombing versus torpedo attack: 'It's much more effective to let water in through the bottom than air through the top.'

In the event, as is well known, the Munich crisis ended by Britain and France buying time at the cost of Czechoslovakia's independence. The plan for attack on the Italian naval base at Taranto was put back in the safe, where it remained until events once again called for its reconsideration.

PART I

Chapter 1

The Mediterranean
1939–1940

——⚓——

In September 1939 Hitler's savage assault on Poland, the independence of which Britain and France had guaranteed, made war with Germany inevitable, but Mussolini, for all his braggadocio and sabre-rattling, opted for neutrality, thus raising faint hopes in diplomatic quarters that he would prefer discretion to valour. In consequence, the British Mediterranean fleet which, on the outbreak of war, comprised three battleships, one aircraft carrier, three 8in (203mm) gun cruisers and three 6in (152mm) gun cruisers, an A/A cruiser, 26 destroyers, four escort vessels, ten submarines and four minesweepers, found itself being gradually milked of ships in order to meet other commitments.

However, following Germany's successful attack on France and Italy's assumption of an increasingly threatening posture, it became imperative to reconstitute this fleet in order to ensure the containment of the Italian fleet and the control of the eastern basin. The situation was aggravated when, after Mussolini's declaration of war on 10 June, eleven days later France signed an armistice with the Axis powers and the French fleet ceased to be available for ensuring the security of the western basin. Another force had therefore to be assembled in haste at Gibraltar, known as Force 'H', to take over this responsibility. Moreover, during the early months of the war, Britain had lost two of the six carriers with which she began the war, and of the four remaining, only one, the *Ark Royal*, was a modern ship. This deplorable situation was only mitigated by the knowledge that new carriers, the construction of which was referred to earlier, were shortly coming in to service.

In repositioning the fleet to meet the new situation, resulting from a hostile Italy, the Admiralty allocated the carrier *Eagle* to the reconstituted Mediterranean fleet commanded by that redoubtable Scot and magnificent leader Admiral Sir Andrew Cunningham. She joined his flag from eastern waters towards the end of May 1940. But even though the Italian fleet lacked aircraft carriers, Italy's geographical position in the central Mediterranean enabled her fleet to operate over a wide area under cover of the shore-based aircraft of the Regia Aeronautica whereas Admiral Cunningham had only the *Eagle*'s eighteen Swordfish TSR aircraft to pit against the enemy's entire air force. These were later supplemented by three Gladiator fighters, and, in the absence of pilots trained to fly them, the *Eagle*'s Commander (Flying), Commander C.L. Keighley-Peach, RN, and two volunteer Swordfish pilots trained by him, successfully kept the Regia Aeronautica at bay until the arrival of HMS *Illustrious*. It was not possible, at that time, to count on any air support from the fortress of Malta, the pre-war planners having written it off as indefensible, a policy only reversed literally at the eleventh hour, but too late to be of any use at this stage.

The Chiefs of Staff of the Italian Armed Forces were given their first intimation that 'il Duce' had decided to enter the war on the side of Germany, whenever he considered the moment opportune, on 9 April 1940. The Chief of the Italian Naval Staff was Admiral Domenico Cavagnari who also held the post of Under Secretary of State for the Navy. Had he not been extremely able and a prodigious worker, he would not have been able to wear these two hats as successfully as he did. Unfortunately for him policy was formulated by the Supreme Command, dominated by Mussolini and the Army, neither of whom understood the conduct of maritime warfare. Cavagnari replied to Mussolini's intended declaration of war in a memorandum of some length. He pointed out the difficulties arising from his country's unfavourable geographical position and the impossibility of achieving any sort of surprise action when entering a war already in an advanced stage. He foresaw that Britain and France would either take up positions at each end of the Mediterranean and await Italy's exhaustion or they would adopt a more aggressive strategy leading to encounters between the opposing fleets, in which substantial losses would be incurred by both sides. Assuming they adopted the first alternative, it would be difficult to carry out offensive operations with surface forces and, as regards to submarine warfare, poor results were likely since merchant shipping in the Mediterranean would be virtually non existent. The outcome of the second course of action would be that, while the Allies could replace their losses from ships surplus to their needs, Italy could not and the fleet would thus be thrown on the defensive and all possibility of pursuing important strategic objectives designed to defeat the opposing naval forces would be forfeited. This led him to the conclusion that a decision to enter the war did not seem justified given the prospect of being obliged to adopt a defensive maritime strategy.

He went on to state the factors adverse to the operation of Italian naval forces which were (a) the shortage of reconnaissance aircraft and the difficulty of having to rely on the co-operation of the Air Force and (b) the poor state of the anti-aircraft defences at the naval bases. He concluded his memorandum with these prescient words: 'Whatever character the war in the Mediterranean assumes, in the end our naval losses will be substantial. In the subsequent peace negotiations Italy would emerge not only without territorial pledges, but also minus a fleet and perhaps an Air Force.'[1] In this realistic way he forecast the course of events as regards the Italian Navy during the forthcoming conflict.

Like the British Admiralty in London, the Italian Naval High Command had a well equipped Operations Room in the Ministry of Marine, known as Supermarina, to which access was only obtainable by holders of a special pass. It was linked with all the naval commands in Italy and Sicily by a rapid communications network which functioned throughout the twenty-four hours and was capable of handling a very large number of incoming and outgoing messages satisfactorily. On large maps were shown the position of all Italian warships and merchant ships, as well as those of any enemy ships reported or the position of which could be deduced from intercepted British messages. Like the German Navy, the Royal Italian Navy began the war with a great advantage, conferred by the ability to decipher British naval messages. In view of the inadequacy of the air reconnaissance provided by the Regia Aeronautica, this was often the only intelligence available of the movements of British ships.

In June 1940, the Italian fleet comprised the two modernised battleships *Giulio Cesare* and *Conte di Cavour*, each armed with ten 12.6in (320mm) guns, nineteen cruisers, seven of which were armed with 8in (203mm) and twelve with 6in (152mm) guns, 61 fleet destroyers, 69 destroyers and torpedo boats, 105 submarines and a number of minelayers, patrol vessels, and motor torpedo boats. Two old battleships, *Caio Duilio* and *Andrea Doria*, were undergoing modernisation and two new ones being completed. Italy had an agreement with her Axis partner, Germany, that each country's Navy would have complete liberty of action it its own theatre of operations. Mussolini followed up his declaration of war on 10 June 1940 with a directive calling for 'the offensive at all points in the Mediterranean and outside.' However Admiral Cavagnari held to his original concept of pursuing a defensive policy. This, he defined as closing the Adriatic and Tyrrhenian Seas to enemy forces and the maintenance of the important line of communications between metropolitan Italy and both Libya and the Dodecanese islands in the Aegean. At the same time, he envisaged offensive raids by high speed forces against French lines of communication with North Africa, possible attacks by high speed torpedo crafts on ships in harbour and mine-laying off enemy ports. Until France withdrew from the conflict on 22 June, the combined Anglo-French fleets in the Mediterranean were superior to that of Italy except in destroyers and submarines, but afterwards, the need for some of the tasks envisaged by Cavagnari was eliminated. Nevertheless, there was no change in the general policy cited above, although there was a notable increase in activity, especially in the number of convoys being despatched to Libya.

Even though the Army had originally said that it had sufficient supplies in Libya for six months, as soon as the fighting started, urgent requests poured in for all kinds of stores and equipment. These convoys generally had a strong escort of destroyers and a covering force of battleship and cruisers. In July, during one of these operations, an encounter took place with the British Mediterranean fleet under Admiral Cunningham, during which a 15in shell fired by HMS *Warspite*, struck the battleship *Giulio Cesare*, flying the flag of Admiral Inigo Campioni, Commander-in-Chief of the Italian fleet, causing severe damage. As a result of this he broke off the action and returned to port, taking advantage of his superior speed. Campioni complained that he had not received sufficient support from the Regia Aeronautica. Reconnaissance had proved inadequate and the results of the bombing attacks on the British fleet, during which no hits were obtained, were most disappointing, especially since, at the time, it was without fighter aircraft defence. To make matters worse, the Italian ships themselves had been attacked by their own aircraft, despite every possible means being used to disclose their identity. The operations are described at some length in the Italian Official History. What impressed their Naval Staff most was the advantage conferred on the British fleet by the presence of an aircraft carrier, which 'besides permitting them to fight off the activities of our aircraft, both bombers and reconnaissance, allowed the enemy to carry out attacks with torpedo aircraft, which, although frustrated by ships manoeuvring, interfered with the formations attacked and so delayed their rejoining the remainder of our forces.'[2]

A further blow to Italian morale was administered ten days later, when, on 19 July, HMAS *Sydney* and a division of destroyers encountered two 6in gun cruisers, the *Giovanni delle Bande Nere*, flying the flag of Vice Admiral F. Casardi, and the *Bartolomeo Colleoni*. The last named was sunk after a spirited action, in which the only damage received by the British force was a hit on the *Sydney*'s funnel. Admiral Casardi was taken by surprise, since he was expecting air reconnaissance from the Dodecanese islands, which did not materialise, and he had not ordered either ship's aircraft to be catapulted *in lieu* to carry out a dawn reconnaissance of the area ahead of his two ships. Captain Novaro of the *Colleoni* was rescued, although, seriously wounded, he died subsequently at Alexandria, where he was buried with full military honours.

On 2 August the Italian fleet was reinforced by the arrival of the two new battleships, *Vittorio Veneto* and *Littorio*, each with a main armament of nine 15in (381mm) guns, which could outrange all the 15in gun battleships in the British fleet except for the *Warspite* and *Valiant*, which had been modernised. The Italian ships were also much faster. At the end of August the work of modernising the *Caio Duilio* was completed and so, on 31 August, Admiral Campioni took his fleet to sea. It comprised two new and three modernised battleships accompanied by ten cruisers and 34 destroyers. Its object was the interception of an inferior British force comprising two battleships, the carrier *Eagle*, five light cruisers and nine destroyers. The British force was covering a convoy from Alexandria to Malta and, at the same time, meeting the long awaited reinforcements from England, which included the new carrier, HMS *Illustrious*, and the battleship *Valiant*. The two fleets approached to within 90 miles of each other at dusk on 31 August and Admiral

Cunningham regarded action at dawn the next day as certain. However, to his surprise, Campioni reversed the course of his fleet during the night and returned to his base at Taranto. His action is explained by Commander Bragadin as being due to a severe storm which blew up during the night and which prevented reconnaissance aircraft from obtaining any information on the position of any of the British forces. It also made the going heavy on his destroyers, which, in any event, were running short of fuel, and so, in the afternoon of September 1st, the Italian High Command, Supermarina, ordered all ships to return to base.[3]

The newly commissioned carrier, HMS *Illustrious*, was a valuable addition to Admiral Cunningham's fleet. She was commanded by Captain (later Admiral Sir Denis) Boyd, DSC, RN, a senior officer of great experience who had earned his decoration while serving as a Lieutenant in the light cruiser, HMS *Fearless*, which led the First Destroyer Flotilla into action at the Battle of Jutland during the First World War. Although a torpedo specialist, he had taken a keen interest in naval aviation throughout his career and, as a young officer, had privately learned to fly. A man of medium height, he was possessed of great physical and moral courage and quickly gained the complete confidence of his ship's company. The *Illustrious* was of a new design of carrier with an armoured flight deck and included, amongst her complement of aircraft, twelve fighters, four of which were new eight gun Fairey Fulmars. Her strike aircraft comprised two squadrons, each of twelve Swordfish TSR aircraft. However, despite this addition to the strength of his carrier-borne aircraft, Admiral Cunningham described the air situation as 'unsatisfactory' because of the lack of reconnaissance aircraft capable of monitoring the movements of the Italian fleet. The flying boats operating from Malta and Alexandria 'were too slow and too vulnerable' he had recorded. 'The Italians, on the other hand, had full knowledge of our movements.'[4] The *Illustrious* reached Gibraltar on 29 August and sailed the following day to rendezvous with Admiral Cunningham's fleet south of Malta. She was flying the flag of Rear Admiral Lumley Lyster, former Captain of HMS *Glorious*, who had been appointed Rear Admiral, Aircraft Carriers, Mediterranean. It is not surprising that, on hoisting his flag, Lyster should have instructed his staff to examine anew the plan he had drawn up two years previously for an attack on the Italian fleet at Taranto. By the time he reached

Alexandria he had refreshed his memory with the details and was in a position to discuss the operation with his Commander-in-Chief.

During the month of August the first aircraft to be equipped with torpedoes joined the Italian Air Force. The war had already demonstrated their value and at long last the pleadings of the Navy were heeded. There were, however, only about fifty of them and the training of the crews took some time. Although they were very much an arm calling for close naval co-operation they were placed under Air Force control.

On 13 September, Marshal Graziani, Commander-in-Chief of the Italian force in North Africa, launched an offensive with the object of invading Egypt, and this kept the British fleet busy supporting the defending army. However, to everyone's surprise, having reached Sidi Barrani, the Marshal halted his forces and instructed them to dig in. The Royal Navy, thus released from its task, was able to give consideration to other pressing matters, included in which was the attack on the Italian fleet at its base. Meanwhile, an essential requirement of such an attack had been met, that of adequate and continuous reconnaissance of Taranto harbour, including photographs from which the scale of the defences could be determined. A week after the *Illustrious* had joined the fleet, three American built Glenn Martyn aircraft, later known as Marylands, reached Malta and took over reconnaissance duties from the Sunderland flying boats. These aircraft were part of a consignment ordered by France in the United States for use as long range bomber/reconnaissance aircraft. They were crated and on their way when France fell, and fortunately redirected to England, where they were turned over to the Royal Air Force, which, lacking any really high speed aircraft of this type, was delighted to have them. Since the War Cabinet considered Admiral Cunningham's need to be the greatest, the first three to be assembled were ordered to form No. 431 General Reconnaissance flight and to proceed to Malta, after familiarisation and night flying trials which were carried out under great difficulty because of enemy air activity. The flight commander was Squadron Leader E.A. Whitely, an experienced and capable pilot, well endowed with the qualities of resourcefulness and courage which work of this nature calls for. On arrival at Luqa, one of Malta's battle-scared airfields, they were immediately assigned to the task of photographing ports in Italy and Sicily, as far north as Naples and as far east as Brindisi, as well as searching for enemy shipping on the supply route between Italy and ports in North Africa, and also in the Ionian Sea. In addition, they were ordered to pay daily visits to enemy naval bases, especially at Taranto.

The art of photographic interpretation was not fully developed until the latter stages of the Second World War, but shortly before the *Illustrious* joined the Mediterranean fleet, RAF Middle East Command in Cairo had set up an interpretation unit. The photographs taken by the Marylands were therefore flown there for study. Admiral Lyster's Assistant Staff Officer Operations, Lieutenant David Pollock, RNVR, obtained permission to undergo a five-day course with this unit, when his ship first reached Alexandria. His peace time profession was that of lawyer, but his favourite hobby was sailing, a combination admirably suited to the duties on which he now found himself engaged. He furnished himself with a stereoscope by means of which two pictures of the same area, when placed side by side and examined through it, produced a three dimensional effect. Taking into account shadows, these enabled an observer to deduce information not noticeable on an ordinary photograph. The knowledge he acquired during this short course was to prove invaluable later on.

At the end of September, another and less favourable opportunity occurred for Admiral Campioni to bring the British fleet to action, when a force comprising the two modernised battleships, *Warspite* and *Valiant*, with the aircraft carrier *Illustrious* in company, once again sailed into the central Mediterranean during an operation designed to cover troop reinforcements for Malta. The force was sighted off Sidi Barrani and Admiral Campioni sailed to intercept it with a force of four battleships, which included the *Littorio* and *Vittorio Veneto*. However, air reconnaissance failed to locate the British force until the afternoon of 1 October, when it was seen to be heading back for its base at Alexandria. Aircraft from the carrier had sighted the Italian ships 120 miles to the north, but as the primary object of the British force on this occasion was the safe arrival of the troops at Malta, it did not seek action with the Italian fleet, which returned to base. Soon afterwards, the whole British fleet returned to the area while covering a supply convoy to Malta, but this time the Italian reaction was to send out a small force of destroyers to carry out a night torpedo attack on the British fleet. They made contact with the 6in gun cruiser *Ajax*, which sank three of them and damaged a fourth while receiving seven shell hits, none of which caused serious damage.

Although, during the first five months of the war with Italy, the British fleet or detachments of it, made some sixteen sweeps into the central Mediterranean from its base at Alexandria, the only encounters with the Italian fleet were those mentioned above. However, the generally defensive policy adopted by the Italian fleet enabled it to dominate the waters around Malta, and not only made it more difficult for supplies to reach the beleaguered island, but also hindered the attempts of British forces to impede the passage of the Italian convoys carrying much needed supplies to their armies in North Africa. Logical though this policy was, it had one inevitable consequence, that of heightening the morale of the British fleet in a way that nothing else could have done, and to the extent that it was ready and willing to overcome the quite formidable problems involved in attacking the Italian fleet lying in its strongly defended base of Taranto.

Chapter 2

Operation Mike Bravo Ate
(MB.8)

—⚏—

Whenever the opportunity arose, the air crews of the two carriers, *Illustrious* and *Eagle*, carried out intensive training including night flying in order to equip themselves for the hazardous enterprise, which they were certain they would shortly be called upon to undertake. By mid October, Lyster was able to report to the Commander-in-Chief that he considered they were sufficiently well trained, and it was decided that the attack should take place on Trafalgar Day, 21 October. However, an unfortunate mishap onboard the *Illustrious* necessitated a postponement. Down in the ship's hangar long-range tanks were being fitted to the Swordfish aircraft to increase the distance at which they could be launched from their objective. As already mentioned, these aircraft had a range of only 450 miles, which was insufficient since it was desirable that the attack should be delivered from a position in which the carrier was unlikely to be detected. As a result, a 60 gallon tank was being secured by metal straps in the Observer's seat in each torpedo-carrying aircraft. This meant that the air gunner had to be left behind and the Observer himself, besides being seriously inconvenienced, ran the risk of being drenched with petrol from the tank overflow pipe as the aircraft accelerated for the take off. One of the fitters on the job suddenly slipped and fell, and, in so doing, the screwdriver which he was clutching brushed across a pair of live electric terminals in the aircraft's cockpit. The spark ignited some petrol dripping from a tank which had not been properly drained and started a fire which spread swiftly to the surrounding aircraft. Fire-fighting parties leapt into action, the overhead spray extinguishers of the drenching system were switched on and in a few minutes the blaze died down. However, brief though it had been, the incident had serious repercussions. Two of the Swordfish were destroyed and five others had been drenched with salt water. It was at once evident, that, even if they worked around the clock, it would not be possible to ready the two Swordfish squadrons by the chosen date.

As every experienced commander knows, the unexpected permeates all operations of war, and on top of the situation described above, Admiral Cunningham now had to face a more serious one. On 28 October, Italy delivered an ultimatum to Greece, the terms of which were rejected by that country, which appealed to Britain for help. Immediate steps were taken to respond to this request and Admiral Cunningham was instructed to establish a fuelling base for the fleet and for aircraft at Suda Bay in Crete, whence troops and stores could be assembled and transported to the port of Piraeus. Italian attempts to interfere with these measures were unsuccessful but their implementation added to the other tasks which the Mediterranean fleet was called upon to undertake at this time. These included the escort of convoys to and from Malta and the passage through the Mediterranean of reinforcements comprising a battleship, two cruisers and three destroyers, all of which had embarked military personnel for the garrison of Malta.

Reconnaissance of Taranto harbour on 27 October had revealed that the Italian main fleet was there. It comprised five battleships, three 8in gun cruisers, six 6in gun cruisers and a number of destroyers. It was therefore well placed to interfere with operations which the British forces were now about to undertake and to which the code name of Mike Bravo Ate (MB.8) was given. It is an indication of Admiral Cunningham's ability to size up his opponent's reaction that the final phase of this complex operation was to be the postponed attack on the Italian fleet in Taranto harbour. The conditions of moonlight were favourable for this any night between 11 and 19 November. It might well be thought that so much activity in the central Mediterranean would have sent the Italian fleet hurrying out to sea to do battle with an enemy, who had the temerity to intrude again on what Mussolini regarded as his exclusive preserve, but, as will be seen, the British Commander-in-Chief's intuition was to be proved right and 'Judgement', the code name given to that particular part of the operation, was singularly apt.

Before sailing to carry out Operation MB.8, another unforeseen event necessitated an amendment to that part of it dealing with the intended attack on Taranto. The 22 year-old carrier *Eagle*, as a result of the bombing attacks and near misses to which she had been subjected during the July operations, developed a serious defect in her petrol supply system. Only a major refit in a dockyard could make this good and so there was no question of her being able to take part in the operation. It was therefore decided that she should transfer five of her Swordfish aircraft and eight complete crews to the *Illustrious* to give her a striking force of 24 aircraft. This was six less than originally planned, but, as will be related later, an accident caused the number to be still further reduced.

Meanwhile, Rear Admiral Lyster had despatched Lieutenant Pollock in a Swordfish aircraft to Cairo to obtain the latest intelligence on the situation at the Italian naval base. A series of excellent photographs covering the entire harbour were available, from which the positions of the battleships, cruisers and destroyers lying there could be noted, and also those of the gun emplacements ashore, established for their defence. However, what at first puzzled the Admiral's staff officer was a series of small white blobs on all the prints, and which were clearly not blemishes. Together with the Royal Air Force expert, Flight Lieutenant John Jones, he examined and re-examined them- then an idea struck him- could the mysterious spots be barrage balloons like those being used for the defence of London? In planning Operation 'Judgement' no allowance had been made for obstructions of this kind; the method of attack would therefore need to be revised if his guess was correct. First, it was necessary to acquaint both Admiral Lyster and the Commander-in-Chief with his suspicions, but the Royal Air Force could not see its way to part with the photographs. Pollock was not a man to be outdone, and so when no one was looking, he 'borrowed' them for 24 hours, hoping they would not be missed. Back at Alexandria he showed them to Admiral Cunningham's Chief of Staff, Rear Admiral (later Admiral of the Fleet Sir Algernon) Willis, who agreed with his interpretation of the new hazard. He then returned to the *Illustrious* to have the pictures copied and the following day he flew back to Cairo and replaced the unmissed photos in their folder. After requesting that official confirmation of this important piece of intelligence be sent to the Commander-in-Chief, he returned onboard his ship to await events. In due course, the report came through, but, thanks to the advance information he had obtained, a revised plan of attack had already been prepared for submission to Admiral Cunningham before the fleet left harbour.

The magnitude of Operation MB.8 can be gauged from the fact that it involved six separate forces totalling five battleships, two carriers, ten cruisers, thirty destroyers and three trawlers. The second carrier was the *Ark Royal* belonging to Force 'H' based on Gibraltar, flying the flag of Vice Admiral Sir James Somerville, but which could not take part in the attack on Taranto, since she was required to provide air cover for the passage of ships through the western basin of the Mediterranean. There were four convoys to be escorted: the first was MW3, of five merchant ships, from Alexandria to Malta, to which three ships were added, loaded with guns and ammunition for the base at Suda Bay. The second one, AN6, comprised three ships carrying petrol and fuel from Egypt to Greece; the third one, ME3, contained four ships returning empty from Malta to Alexandria, while the fourth one included empty ships returning to Alexandria from Greece and Turkey. During the operation, the battleship, *Barham*, with the cruisers *Berwick* and *Glasgow* were to be escorted from Gibraltar by Force 'H' to rendezvous with Admiral Cunningham south of Malta as reinforcements for his fleet.

The operation was timed to commence on 4 November with the sailing of convoy AN6 from Alexandria. The following day, the Malta bound convoy, MW3, sailed and overtook AN6 off the southern entrance to the Kaso Strait. As they passed through it and north of Crete, the two ships for Suda Bay were detached en route, and from there, through a position 40 miles south of Cape Matapan, the convoy steered for its destination. Admiral Cunningham, in the battleship *Warspite* with the *Valiant*, *Malaya*, *Ramillies*, the carrier *Illustrious*, the cruisers *Gloucester* and *York* and an escort of destroyers, sailed from Alexandria at 1300 on 6 November and steered to the west. By noon on the 8th, the fleet was halfway between Crete and Malta, when convoy MW3 was sighted, ten miles to the south-west. The fleet took station to the north, in order to be in a position to intercept any Italian warship attempting to attack it. At 1230, MW3 was sighted by Italian reconnaissance aircraft, which were driven off by fighters launched from the *Illustrious*. The fleet had now approached to within 180 miles of Sicily and air attacks could be expected at any time. Another reconnaissance aircraft appeared at 1520 but was chased away by the vigilant fighters. About an hour later seven S.79 bombers appeared and were attacked by three Fulmar fighters, which shot down two, whereupon the remaining five jettisoned their bombs and made off. At 0900/9 the battleship *Ramillies* was detached with an escort of three destroyers to accompany the convoy to Malta, while the rest of the fleet proceeded to a covering position about 100 miles to the south-east of the island. The cruisers were ordered to sweep northward and search for enemy forces as the weather was too overcast for air searches to be relied upon. During the latter part of the forenoon and the afternoon, enemy aircraft were reported in the vicinity of the fleet four times and at 1604 a Cant 506 shadowing aircraft was shot down by a Fulmar. The Italians, now aware of the presence of British forces to the west and east of Malta, were trying unsuccessfully to obtain a picture of the situation. On 9 November, Commander Bragadin says 'it was learned that the Gibraltar force had reversed course in keeping with the now classic British operational procedure. As far as the eastern squadron was concerned, the reconnaissance service gave various and conflicting reports. By that evening Supermarina could only conclude, in a general way, that this British force must have been about 300 miles from Taranto and on its way to Alexandria at approximately 1500 that afternoon.'[5] The mistake was not discovered until the following day.

Meanwhile, at 1219 the *Illustrious* had launched a Swordfish aircraft on a routine anti-submarine patrol, but shortly after taking off, the engine failed and it force landed in the sea, close to the *Warspite*, the crew being rescued by a destroyer. At 0700/10 another Swordfish, launched to carry out reconnaissance of a sector between north-west and north-east from the fleet, crashed soon after take off. Although the crew was rescued, the aircraft was lost, reducing the number available for the attack on Taranto to 22. Three hours later the battleship *Barham* and her two accompanying cruisers were met, the latter being detached to land the troops they were carrying, at Malta. At noon, in a position some 40 miles west of that island, enemy aircraft again made contact with the fleet and one of them, a Cant 501, was shot down. At 1330 ten enemy bombers attacked the fleet in two formations from a height of 14,000ft (4,297m) and dropped 25 bombs without scoring a hit. They were intercepted by the *Illustrious*'s Fulmars and one was damaged. The fleet now turned east and, at noon/11, had returned to a position about halfway between Malta and Crete, but meanwhile another Swordfish had mysteriously crashed. It had climbed to 1,500ft (457m) when the engine cut out without warning and it landed in the sea. The Pilot, Sub Lieutenant Alistair Keith and his Observer, Lieutenant George Going, managed to inflate their life-saving dinghy and climb into it before being rescued by a boat from the cruiser *Gloucester*. Going, who has been described to the author by an officer who knew him as 'the bravest man I ever met' suddenly realised that unless he could get back to the *Illustrious*, he would miss the raid on Taranto. He went up to the cruiser's bridge to put the matter before the Captain who proved sympathetic and gave orders for the ship's amphibious Walrus aircraft to be catapulted off and return the two aviators to their ship.

Commander James Robertson, RN, the Commander (Flying) onboard the carrier, known to his shipmates as 'Streamline' for his remarkable ability to speed up any operation connected with the handling of aircraft, was determined to discover the reason for the loss of the three Swordfish in such unusual circumstances. They all belonged to Number 819 squadron and this suggested contamination of the fuel rather than individual engine failures. He ordered the tanks of the remaining nine aircraft of the squadron to be drained immediately and the fuel examined. This done, it was found to contain water and sand mixed in with the petrol as well as a peculiar fungus type growth festooning the baffles in the tanks. Further inquiry elicited the fact that they had all been refuelled from the same supply point in the hangar and this pointed to contamination of one of the ship's tanks. This, he surmised, might well be the result of the action necessary to extinguish the fire, or possibly some other cause. However, whatever it might have been, the important thing was to have discovered it and to have been able to prevent what would have been little short of a disaster so far as the impending attack on Taranto was concerned.

It had been arranged that simultaneously with the attack on the Italian fleet base, light forces under the command of Vice Admiral Pridham-Wippell should carry out a sweep into the mouth of the Adriatic. This force was detached to proceed in execution of previous orders at 1310/11 and at 1800 the *Illustrious*, escorted by the cruisers *Gloucester*, *Berwick*, *Glasgow* and *York*, also separated from the main body of the fleet preparatory to the launching of Operation 'Judgement'.

Chapter 3

The Plan of Attack

—✺—

The port of Taranto, at the head the Gulf of that name, is situated in the heel of Italy, 520 miles from Malta. It was the Italian fleet's premier base and contained all the facilities necessary to support ships of all types. It comprised an Inner Harbour known as Mar Piccolo, completely landlocked, to which access was obtained thorough a narrow channel called the Canal, and a large Outer Harbour known as Mar Grande. The latter was enclosed by a submerged breakwater extending south-west from Cape Rondinella to the island of San Pietro and continuing thence to the Isolotto San Paolo, which marked the northern side of the 1,298yd (1,187m) wide entrance. To the south, a breakwater, known as the Diga di San Vito, extended north-east for 1,760yds (1,609m) from a position on shore 1,319yds (1,206m) north-east of the Cape of that name. The Italian High Command was well aware of the possibility of an air attack on the harbour and had taken extensive precautions to protect the ships within it. These included the positioning of 21 batteries of 4in (102mm) guns, thirteen of which were ashore and eight mounted on floating rafts. There were also 84 heavy and 109 light machine guns sited to cover the whole area of the port. Although perhaps adequate in number, the batteries consisted of out of date weapons and they were not equipped for night barrage fire. The 22 searchlights were modern but only two of them were linked with the airphonic listening posts, of which thirteen had been established in suitable positions in the country surrounding the harbour area. Additional illumination was to be provided by two searchlights from each ship. Of the 13,998yds (12,800m) of anti torpedo net defence required to protect the ships in the Outer Harbour only 4,593yds (4,200m) were in position; a further 3,171yds (2,900m) was ashore waiting to be laid. The fact that this had not been done was due to objections by some senior naval officers who believed that they would interfere with the movements of ships entering and leaving harbour. To complete this quite imposing array of defences, a barrage of some 90 balloons had been installed, but, as luck would have it, bad weather during the first week in November had destroyed 60 of them and only 27 were in position on the night of the attack. Ten were moored to rafts just west of an inner breakwater, known as the Diga di Tarantola, which jutted out into the Mar Grande for 2,625yds (2,400m) and about the same distance to the north-east of the Diga di San Vito. A further ten were sited ashore in a line extending north-east from the inshore end of the Diga di Tarantola and the remaining seven were moored to rafts in the middle of the northern half of the Mar Grande on a line running north-east towards the northern shore of the harbour (see plan 1). There was, however, one serious lacuna in the defences, and that was the absence of any smoke-making apparatus.

On 11 November the following ships of the Italian fleet were moored in Taranto harbour. In the Mar Grande, the two 15in (381mm) gun battleships, *Vittorio Veneto* and *Littorio*, and the four 12.6in (320mm) gun battleships, *Cavour*, *Giulio Cesare*, *Caio Duilio* and *Andrea Doria*. The last named ship had been unable to recover her stern moorings on her return to harbour. Also present were the 8in (240mm) gun cruisers *Zara*, *Fiume* and *Gorizia*, and the destroyers, *Folgare*, *Baleno*, *Fulmine*, *Lampo*, *Alfieri Gioberti*, *Carducci* and *Oriani*. In the Mar Piccolo, at buoys, were the 8in (204mm) gun cruisers *Trieste* and *Bolzano* and the destroyers, *Granatiere*, *Alpino*, *Bersagliere* and *Fuciliere*, while moored stern to the jetty were the 8in (204mm) gun cruisers *Pola* and *Trento*. In addition, there were the 6in (154mm) gun cruisers *Garibaldi* and *Abruzzi*, and the destroyers *Freccia*, *Strale*, *Dardo*, *Saetta*, *Maestrale*, *Libeccio*, *Grecale*, *Scirocco*, *Camicia Nera*, *Geniere*, *Lanciere*, *Carabiniere*, *Corazziere*, *Ascari*, *Da Recco*, *Usodimare*, and *Pessagno*. Also in the Inner Harbour were five torpedo boats, sixteen submarines, four minesweepers, one minelayer, nine tankers, supply ships and hospital ships as well as some tugs and merchant ships.

The ships were berthed in a manner considered to afford them the best protection from the kind of attack considered likely. The repeated visits by the British reconnaissance aircraft had not passed unnoticed and were regarded as an indication that air attacks were being planned. As a result, at nightfall ships assumed a state of complete readiness with main armaments half manned and A/A guns fully so. In the event of an alarm, all men on watch had orders to take cover while those not on duty were to proceed below.

The Admiral in charge of the port was Arturo Riccardi, a man who took his responsibilities very seriously. He fully appreciated the risk of an air-borne torpedo attack on the ships lying in the Outer Harbour, but he counted on receiving adequate warning of the approach of hostile aircraft. He believed that a carrier approaching within striking distance was almost certain to be sighted by reconnaissance aircraft before she could reach a position from which she would be able to launch her aircraft. The Italian Army, on the other hand, which was responsible for the A/A batteries, was less confident about the security of the base and would have been glad to see the fleet move to one further north, such as Naples. Admiral Campioni, however, was reluctant to forego the strategic advantages of Taranto *vis-à-vis* his hope of cutting off the supplies with which, despite his efforts, the British were managing to keep Malta going.

The original plan of attack on Taranto, as conceived by Rear Admiral Lyster, had had to be considerably modified as a result of the discovery of the barrage balloons, the anti-torpedo nets, the fewer aircraft available due to the *Eagle* not being present and finally the loss of three more Swordfish, as related above. In its final form, the plan was as follows: the *Illustrious* and her escort of cruisers and destroyers would steer for a position 'X', 270° 4 miles from Kabbo Point, Cephalonia, in order to pass through it at 2000 on 11 November. This early hour had been chosen to minimise the risk of attack by surface craft, which was considered to be greater than that of detection by reconnaissance aircraft, which, as events were to prove, were hardly ever allowed to approach the fleet by the vigilant Fleet Air Arm fighters. Since only 21 Swordfish aircraft were available instead of the 30 previously envisaged, they were organised in two flights of twelve and nine aircraft respectively, six of which in each flight were armed with torpedoes and the remainder with bombs. The first strike of twelve aircraft would be launched on reaching position 'X', which was so chosen that the aircraft would not have to fly more than a total distance of 400 miles. Since the balloon barrage and the anti-torpedo nets restricted the number of favourable dropping positions, the bombing aircraft would be equipped with flares. The second strike of nine aircraft would be launched an hour after the first one, i.e. at 2100. It was hoped to commence the recovery of the first strike at about 0100/12 in a position 20 miles 270° from Kabbo Point. Moonrise was at 1543 and at 2300 it would bear 197° at an altitude of 52° as seen from Taranto. The first strike was to fly up the centre of the Gulf and approach the harbour from the south-west. The six bombing aircraft would illuminate the target area by dropping flares along its eastern edge before proceeding to bomb the cruisers and destroyers lying in the Mar Piccolo.

This, in broad outline, was the plan as given to the Pilots and Observers onboard the *Illustrious* and on which the respective Squadron Commanders then proceeded to work out, in greater detail, the specific method of attack each would adopt.

To carry out an aircraft torpedo attack by day in the open sea is a difficult enough task, as was confirmed on many occasions during the war, but, although a ship in harbour is a sitting duck, if the harbour is well defended and under conditions of darkness, the difficulties are enormously increased. Not only does such an attack call for a cool head and steady nerves, but good judgement is also essential, since reliance has to be placed on the eye as opposed to instruments. The first thing is to identify the target and decide on the method of approach. However thorough the planning and the briefing, this is something which can only be decided on the spur of the moment. The dive down to water level must bring the aircraft to the right place for dropping with a clear range. If there is a balloon barrage, course must be adjusted to miss it or to pass between two of the balloons and no attention must be paid to A/A fire. Reliance cannot be placed on the altimeter in choosing the moment to pull out of a dive, since it suffers from time lag, and so it is a question of experience and making use of the known height of the target to assist one's judgement. The aircraft must be aimed straight at the target and must be level in both axes before the torpedo is released or it will not run straight. Finally, the range at which the torpedo is dropped must not be less than 300yds (275m) as the safety range on the pistol will not have been run off and the warhead will not explode even if a hit is obtained. Just before dropping and when climbing for the getaway, the aircraft is most vulnerable, and since modern warships are capable of devastating close-range fire, the chances of survival cannot be assessed as anything other than poor.

A Swordfish aircraft had been sent to Malta earlier in the day to collect the latest pictures of Taranto taken by the invaluable Maryland reconnaissance aircraft. These, Lieutenant Commanders K.W. Williamson and J.W. Hale, the leaders of the first and second strikes, now began to study carefully. They were excellent photographs, taken on a clear day from a height of only 8,000ft (2,438m) and five Italian battleships could be clearly seen and so could the unwelcome white blobs of the barrage balloons. The fear that the enemy ships might put to sea before the attack took place was allayed when, during the evening, a patrolling Sunderland aircraft keeping watch against this possibility, not only reported that all ships were present and that there was no sign of an impending departure, but also that a sixth battleship had joined the other five. This was indeed good news. Williamson decided on an approach with his squadron to the harbour at a height of between 8 and 10,000ft (2,438-3,048m). He would then glide down with two torpedo-armed aircraft of the leading sub-flight across the Diga di Tarantola from the west, while the other sub-flight would come in from the north-west. By attacking from two directions he hoped to confuse the A/A defences, but in any case each pilot was free to take whatever action the situation demanded, especially should the A/A fire prove more formidable than expected or the balloon barrage interfere with the approach. Hale chose to approach in line astern from the north-west. He estimated that this would give his flight a better run in as well as a more certain chance of hitting, since, from this angle, the battleships overlapped one another. The disadvantage of an approach from the north-west was that his aircraft would have to pass unpleasantly close to the A/A batteries sited on either side of the Canal connecting the Inner and Outer Harbours and they would have to cross the line of barrage balloons moored to lighters to the north-west of their targets. However, on balance, it was considered that these risks were acceptable. The balloons were about 300yds (273m) apart and the wingspan of a Swordfish was less than 48ft (14.6m) so that the chances of passing between two without touching the wires were roughly ten to one in favour.

The average depth of the anchorage where the battleships lay was 49ft (15m) and the torpedoes with which the Swordfish were to be armed and on which the success of the attack depended, were the standard 18in (457mm) Mark XII set to run at 27 knots at a depth of 33ft (10m). They were fitted with Duplex pistols which the *Illustrious* had brought from England and which had only come into service shortly before the outbreak of war. They differed from the ordinary contact pistols in that they included a device actuated by an enemy ship's magnetic field as the torpedo passed underneath her and which fired the primer and exploded the warhead. Since the bottom of a ship is more vulnerable, being less well protected, than the sides, the use of these pistols, it was hoped, would increase the effectiveness of the attack. However, they still had some faults which had not been eliminated when they were brought into service, one of which was a tendency to explode prematurely when running in a swell. Fortunately in the case of the attack on Taranto, such conditions were unlikely to be encountered, but two other problems presented themselves. To minimise the risk of a torpedo being dropped at too steep an angle and hitting the bottom before being able to take up its preset depth, the aircraft must be in level flight or very slight nose down at an altitude of 150ft (45m) when the weapon is released. The depth of water on dropping must not be less than six fathoms (11m) and the distance from the target must be greater than 300yds (274m) as a safety device prevents the pistol from being actuated until the torpedo has run that distance. The first problem could only be overcome by the skill of the Pilot, but the second could be mitigated to some extent by running off some of the safety range before loading the torpedo into the aircraft. Although this entailed a certain amount of risk, it was readily accepted by the aircraft crews.

The bomb-carrying aircraft were armed with six 250lb (112kg) semi-armour piercing bombs, but those detailed for flare dropping only carried four bombs in addition to sixteen flares.

The extent of Operation MB.8 and the number of British forces operating in the Central Mediterranean appears to have confused the enemy. According to Commander Bragadin, who was serving in Supermarina at the time, it was known that both the Gibraltar and Alexandria forces were at sea, the latter reported as comprising three battleships (it was in fact four) and a carrier, and believed to have left their respective bases on 7 November. As a result, the fleet at Taranto had been brought to short notice for steam. The results of air reconnaissance the following morning (8 November) were negative but during the afternoon a convoy was sighted steering towards Malta, outside the range of possible interception. A little later Admiral Cunningham's covering force of battleships was sighted to the south of the convoy, steering south. Nine more submarines in addition to the normal patrols were ordered to the area and a number of motor torpedo boats were ordered to patrol the Malta Channel. Twenty-five bombers took off from Sicilian airfields, but failed to find the British fleet. On 9 November reports indicated that the Gibraltar force was heading back to the west, but those about Admiral Cunningham's force were conflicting and the conclusion was reached that it was on its way back to Alexandria. Some surprise was caused, therefore, when, on the morning of 10 November, reports were received from observation posts on the islands of Pantelleria and Linosa that a group of ships had been sighted, which had evidently broken off from the Gibraltar force and which must have passed through the Sicilian Channel during the night. These ships were the battleship *Barham* with the cruisers *Berwick* and *Glasgow*, with three destroyers, which made a rendezvous with Admiral Cunningham's force at 1015 on that day. In the afternoon an unspecified number and type of ships was reported proceeding east from Malta. This was a convoy of four merchant ships escorted by the battleship *Ramillies*, the A/A cruiser *Coventry* and two destroyers, which had left Malta at 1330 for Alexandria. A group of bombers took off to attack this force but failed to find it. Somewhat ruefully, Commander Bragadin remarks 'If the British had not explained after the war what had gone on in those days, the Italians would not know what these movements had been.'[6]

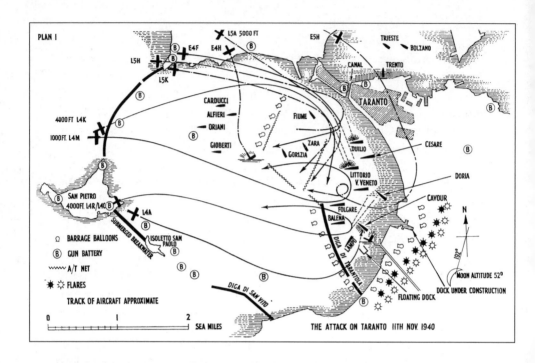

PLAN 1

L5A 5000 FT

E5H

TRIESTE
BOLZANO

L5H E4F E4H

CANAL TRENTO

L5K

B B

TARANTO

CARDUCCI
ALFIERI
ORIANI
GIOBERTI

FIUME

4000 FT L4K

1000 FT L4M

ZARA
GORIZIA

DUILIO

CESARE B

DORIA

CAVOUR

SAN PIETRO
4000 FT L4R/L4G

L4A

LITTORIO
V. VENETO

SUBMERGED BREAKWATER

ISOLETTO SAN
PAOLO

FOLGARE
BALENA

Ω BARRAGE BALLOONS

B GUN BATTERY

〜〜〜 A/T NET

✺ ☼ FLARES

TRACK OF AIRCRAFT APPROXIMATE

DIGA DI TARANTOLA

MOON ALTITUDE 52°

DOCK UNDER CONSTRUCTION

FLOATING DOCK

DIGA DI SAN VITO

0   1   2

SEA MILES

THE ATTACK ON TARANTO 11TH NOV. 1940

192°

N

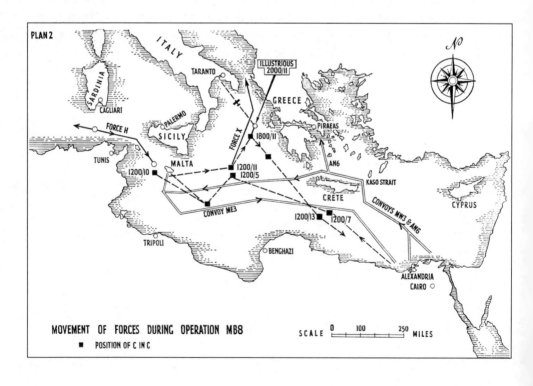

PLAN 2

ITALY

N

SARDINIA

TARANTO

ILLUSTRIOUS
2000/11

GREECE

CAGLIARI

FORCE H

PALERMO
SICILY

FORCE X

1800/11

PIRAEAS

TUNIS

MALTA

1200/10

1200/11
1200/5

AN6

KASO STRAIT

CRETE

CYPRUS

CONVOY ME3

1200/13 1200/7

CONVOYS MW3 & AN6

TRIPOLI

BENGHAZI

ALEXANDRIA
CAIRO

MOVEMENT OF FORCES DURING OPERATION MB8

■ POSITION OF C IN C

SCALE 0   100   250   MILES

Chapter 4

The Attack Goes In

—⁓—

'When detached, Illustrious will adjust course and speed to pass through position 'X' at 2000'- so ran the orders of Rear Admiral Lyster to the carrier's Commanding Officer. They continued: 'On completion of flying off first range, course will be altered 180° to starboard, speed 17 knots and a second alteration of 180° to starboard will be made to pass again through position 'X' at 2100, when course and speed will be adjusted as before.' As the bows of the carrier sliced through the calm Mediterranean sea, flanked on either side by the cruisers *Gloucester*, *Berwick*, *Glasgow* and *York* with four destroyers, down below in the hangar, the aircraft fitters were carrying out final checks on the 21 Swordfish aircraft on which the success or failure of the operation depended. All aircraft are allotted an identification number; those of the *Illustrious* bore the letter 'L' while those lent from the *Eagle* carried the letter 'E'. With their wings folded they presented a curious sight, but this was necessary to enable them to be stowed in the limited space available and accommodated on the lift which carried them up to the flight deck. Before this took place, each Pilot would inspect his aircraft, check the controls, test the torpedo dropping gear and make sure that all the equipment was in full working order. He made sure that the emergency rations were onboard as these were part of the escape plan for any Pilot or Observer who had the misfortune to be shot down. The Observers went up to the Air Intelligence Office for a last minute briefing and a final look at the photographs of the stronghold they were about to attack. To them, as navigators, was assigned the important task of guiding their aircraft during its four-hour flight to and from the target and of finding the carrier again – a tiny dot on a darkened sea. Fortunately they had the black mass of the island of Cephalonia, off which they knew the carrier would be steaming, to help them, and once within 50 miles of the carrier, they should be able to pick up her homing beacon. There was of course the possibility, which could not be allowed for, that the carrier might be intercepted by enemy forces and be unable to make the prearranged rendezvous, but that was an added risk which had to be taken just like that of being shot down, and something to be pushed to the back of the mind and not discussed.

The First Attack

At 1945 the *Illustrious* increased speed to 28 knots and the great ship shuddered, as, down in the engine room, the Artificers on watch opened up the valves, admitting steam to the turbines, while in the boiler rooms additional burners were switched on to generate the extra power required. The Commander (Flying) took up his position in a special sponson just below the bridge from where he had a full view of the darkened flight deck and the dimly discernible figures moving about it. In reply to his querulous enquiry concerning the readiness of the first flight for take off, he was told that there had been a slight delay in fuelling. Then, just as eight bells struck in muffled tones over the ship's broadcasting system, the last of the twelve Swordfish came up the forward lift and was ranged beside the other eleven. The warning klaxons were sounded, engines were switched on, Pilots and Observers, now clad in bulky Sidcot suits and Mae Wests, clambered into their aircraft and fastened their parachute harness with the help of the fitters. Engines were revved up, oil pressures checked, and the readings of the many dials in the cockpit scanned by practised eyes. The Observers put on the earphones of their radio sets and erected their chart boards and navigational equipment. The Intercom with the Pilot was plugged in and communications tested. The flash of a green shaded torch from the leading aircraft told Robertson that it was ready for take off. He passed the information to Captain Boyd who, disguising the intensity of his feelings, gave the order to 'Carry On', in a matter of fact voice. A green light flashed from Flying Control, the fitters and rigger, lying prone on the deck, whipped away the holding chocks and, one by one, the pilots opened their throttles, causing their aircraft to speed along the flight deck, now outlined in fairy lights, and up into the surrounding darkness.

The first disturbance of that quiet November night at Taranto was at 1955, when a diaphonic listening post picked up the sound of aircraft somewhere to the south of the harbour. The information was passed to Command Headquarters, where it did not generate much interest as it could well have been just another reconnaissance aircraft. However, about ten minutes later a number of other airphonic stations began sending in reports of suspicious noises, and so the Fortress Commander was informed and he ordered the Alarm to be sounded. The crews manned their guns while the civilian population hurried down to the air-raid shelters. An A/A battery opened fire but soon ceased and the listening posts reported the sound of aircraft engines to be fading. The intruder appeared to have turned away and after a short pause the All Clear was sounded and peace returned, but not for long.

Three quarters of an hour later further reports came from the airphonic stations on the eastern arm of the Gulf of suspicious noises and another Alarm was sounded. The cause of all the trouble was, in fact, the Sunderland aircraft from Number 228 Squadron, Middle East Command, carrying out its important duty of patrolling the Gulf and watching for any movements on the part of the Italian fleet. Once again the disturbing sounds died away and quiet again descended on the city of Taranto and the darkened ships lying within its capacious harbour.

At 2225 the telephone in Command Headquarters started ringing again and 25 minutes later the sleeping inhabitants were awakened by a third Alarm. As the noise of aircraft engines coming from the south-east intensified, expectancy rose. Suddenly the batteries in the San Vito area erupted in flame while orange and red tracers patterned the sky. The curtain had risen on what will always be remembered by the Italians as 'Taranto Night'.

Flying at a speed of 75 knots and a height of 7,500ft (2,286m), eight of the twelve Swordfish of 815 Squadron had at last risen clear of the cloud in four sub-flight V formations of three aircraft, and the Flight Commander, Williamson, was able to take stock of the situation. The four missing aircraft, which had obviously lost touch during the climb, included one torpedo armed and three bombers. He was not unduly concerned about the last named, whose mission called for independent action anyway, but he sincerely hoped that no misfortune had overtaken the missing torpedo aircraft. The time was 2115 and his Observer, Lieutenant Norman Scarlett, reckoned that there was still an hour and a half to go. At about 2250, Williamson saw the sky ahead illuminated by bursts of gunfire as the batteries guarding Taranto put up a protecting barrage against the unseen enemy aircraft detected approaching, thus confirming visually the accuracy of Scarlett's navigation. Several of the other aircraft crews noted the firework display with which they were being welcomed and deduced that the enemy had not been caught napping.

Williamson and Scarlett, in Aircraft L4A, with Sub Lieutenants Sparke and Neale in aircraft L4C, led the flight up the Gulf of Taranto. The weather was fine and clear with a light surface wind, but at 8,000ft (2,438m) it was westerly 10 knots. The sky was almost fully covered with thin cloud and the moon was three-quarters full, bearing about 190°. As they approached, they spotted the missing torpedo aircraft L4M, piloted by Lieutenant Swayne with Sub Lieutenant Buxall, RNVR, as his Observer. Having lost touch with the remainder, he had made straight for the target and, arriving half an hour early, had passed the time by orbiting above it and keeping the defenders guessing what it was all about. The moment had now come to detach the flare droppers. These were aircraft L4P, with Lieutenant L.J. Kigell, RN, as Pilot and Lieutenant H.R.B. Janvrin, RN, as Observer, and L5B, the Pilot being Lieutenant C.B. Lamb, RN, with Lieutenant K.G. Grieve, RN, as Observer. They were detached to seaward of Cape San Vito, from where a stream of shell intermingled with tracers now began to pour from the batteries. Both aircraft were flying at a height of 7,500ft (2,286m) and at 2302 L4P began dropping a line of magnesium flares at intervals of half a mile in a north-easterly direction, to the south-east of the line of barrage balloons which were protecting the landward side of the anchorage. They were set to burn at 4,500ft (1,371m). Having completed his task satisfactorily, Kigell turned to starboard and, after cruising around for about a quarter of an hour, he made a dive bombing attack on the oil storage depot a quarter of a mile inland from the anchorage, but the results of his mission were not observed. L4P then set course to return to the *Illustrious*. L5B, the stand-by flare dropper, finding that the flares dropped by L4P were functioning correctly, followed the sub-flight leader and joined in the bombing of the oil depot before turning for home.

Williamson, in L4A with L4C and L4R in company, flew to the centre of the Mar Grande. The A/A fire was now intense and appeared to be concentrated in a cone over the centre of the harbour. He put his aircraft into a shallow dive, heading straight for the inferno erupting below him.

He had three and a half miles to go to reach the battleships moored in the eastern part of the harbour. Losing height rapidly, he passed between two of the barrage balloons moored just west of the Diga di Tarantola, narrowly missing one of them, and then on over the breakwater towards the destroyers *Lampo* and *Fulmine*, which engaged him at almost point blank range. Suddenly the massive hull of the battleship *Conte di Cavour* loomed up ahead and Williamson pressed the release button for his torpedo, and the aircraft, relieved of the weight, jerked upwards. He banked steeply to starboard and, as he did so, a burst of automatic machine gun fire ripped into his aircraft, which plummeted straight into the sea. However, his torpedo had found its mark, and a few minutes later the great battleship was shaken by a violent explosion beneath her keel, between the conning tower and 'B' turret. The other two aircraft of the sub-flight, L4C and L4R, crossed the breakwater at a height of only 30ft (9.1m) amidst a hail of fire. They were hoping to attack the *Vittorio Veneto*, but were too far south and, sighting the *Conte di Cavour* they dropped their torpedoes at a range of about 700yds (640m) from her. Unfortunately, they both missed, and the torpedoes ran on to explode simultaneously, close to the battleship *Andrea Doria*, without however damaging her. After dropping, L4C banked sharply to port and both aircraft set course to return to the carrier.

The second sub-flight leader, Lieutenant N. McI. Kemp, RN, in L4K with Sub Lieutenant (A) R.A. Bailey, RN, as his Observer, passed north of San Pietro Island at a height of 4,000ft (1,219m). The batteries, both on the island and on Cape Rondinella to the north, kept up a continuous fire on him, but miraculously his aircraft passed through it unscathed. The enemy battleships close inshore were clearly silhouetted against the light of the slowly descending flares. Diving steeply, Kemp passed around the northern end of the balloon barrage and fortunately, just at that moment, the A/A fire of the nearby cruisers temporarily ceased. Skimming low over the water, he pointed his aircraft at the battleship *Littorio* and, when the range had dropped to an estimated 1,000yds (914m), he released his torpedo. His mission accomplished, he had just time to see the silver streak of his weapon below him heading towards its target, before putting his aircraft into a steep climb, pursued by a hail of tracer bullets. Skilfully avoiding the southern group of barrage balloons, he gained the open sea. His torpedo hit the *Littorio* on her starboard bow.

Swayne, in L4M, who, it will be remembered, had arrived early and had been obliged to await the arrival of the rest of the strike, followed his sub-flight leader, Kemp, in L4K north of San Pietro Island, but at a height of only 1,000ft (305m), and steered straight for the northern end of the breakwater. Intense A/A fire was encountered from the ships and batteries as he crossed the harbour, losing height. On reaching the end of the mole, he made a sharp turn to port and let go his torpedo 400yds (365m) from the *Littorio*, which it struck on the port quarter only a few seconds after a hit obtained by L4K's torpedo on the starboard bow. However, Swayne could not wait to see the results of his attack, and, lifting his aircraft up and over the masts of the battleship, he banked to port and fled from the scene, pursued by a hail of flak.

The last of the torpedo-armed aircraft of the first strike was E4F, with Lieutenant M.R. Maund, RN, as Pilot and Sub Lieutenant (A) W.A. Bull, RN, as Observer. The former, who alas lost his life on 11 January 1943 during air operations off Malta, has left us this dramatic account of his part in the attack.

'Six thousand feet. God, how cold it is here! The sort of cold that fills you until all else is drowned, save perhaps fear and loneliness. Suspended between heaven and earth in a sort of no-man's land – to be sure, no man was ever meant to be here – in the abyss which men of old feared to meet if they ventured to the ends of the earth. Is it surprising that my knees are knocking together? We have now passed under a sheet of alto-stratus cloud which blankets the moon, allowing only a few pools of silver where small gaps appear. And, begob, Williamson is going to climb through it! As the rusty edge is reached I feel a tugging at my port wing, and find that Kemp had edged me over into the slipstream of the leading sub-flight. I fight with hard right stick to keep the wing up, but the sub-flight has run into one of its clawing moments, and quite suddenly the wind and nose drop and we are falling out of the sky! I let her have her head and see the shape of another aircraft flash by close overhead. Turning, I see formation light ahead and climb up after them, following them through one of the rare holes in this cloud mass. There are two aircraft sure enough, yet when I range up alongside, the moon glow shows up the figure 5A – that is Olly [Captain O. Patch]. The others must be ahead. After an anxious few minutes some dim lights appear amongst the upper billows of the cloud, and opening the throttle we lumber away from Olly after them. Poor old engine- she will get a tanning this trip.

'The sub-flight is reassembled now at 8,000 feet. We have come to the edge of the cloud. The regular flashing of a light away down to starboard claims attention. 'There's a flashing light to starboard, Bull, can you place it?' 'Oh, yes' and that is all - the poor devil must be all but petrified with the cold by now.

'Then, the coast appears. Just a band of dull wrinkled greyness. Bull arouses himself from his icicles enough to be able to tell me that we have roughly 40 minutes to go, and I enough to remind him to close the overload tank cock before we go in. But we make no turn to get out to seaward again; instead we shape our course parallel to the coastline, not more than five miles away, giving away in one act any chance of surprise we might have hoped for.

'Years later. Some quaint-coloured twinkling flashes like liver-spots have appeared in the sky to the starboard. It is some time before I realise their significance; we are approaching the harbour; and the flashes are HE shells bursting in a barrage on the target area. We turn towards the coast and drop away into line astern, engines throttled back. For ages we seem to hover without any apparent alteration; then red, white, and green flaming onions come streaming in our direction, the HE bursts get closer, and looking down to starboard I see the vague smudge of a shape I now know as well as my own hand. We are in attacking position. The next ahead disappears as I am looking for my line of approach, so down we go in a gentle pause, glide towards the north-western corner of the harbour. The master switch is made, a notch or two back on the incidence wheel, and my fear is gone, leaving a mind as clear and unfettered as it had ever been in my life. The hail of tracer at 6,000 feet is behind now, and there is nothing here to dodge; then I see that I am wrong, it is not behind anymore. They have shifted target; for now, away to starboard, a hail of red, white, and green balls cover the harbour to a height of 2,000ft. This thing is beyond a joke.

'A burst of brilliance on the north-eastern shore, then another and another as the flare-dropper releases his load, until the harbour shows clear in the light he has made. Not too bright to dull the arc of raining colour over the harbour where tracer flies, allowing, it seems, no room to escape unscathed.

'We are now at 1,000ft over a neat residential quarter of the town where gardens in darkened squares show at the back of the houses marshalled by the neat plan of streets that serve them. Here is the main road that connects the district with the main town. We follow its line and, as I open the throttle to elongate the glide, a Breda swings round from the shore, turning its stream of red balls in our direction. This is the beginning. Then another two guns farther north get our scent – white balls this time – so we throttle back again and make for a black mass on the shore that looks like a factory, where no balloons are likely to grow. A tall factory chimney shows ahead against the water's sheen. We must be at a hundred feet now and soon we must make our dash across that bloody water. As we come abreast the chimney I open the throttle wide and head for the mouth of the Mar Piccolo, whose position, though not visible, can be judged by the lie of the land. Then it is as all hell comes tumbling in on top of us – it must have been the fire of the cruisers and Mar Piccolo Canal batteries – leaving only two things in my mind, the line of approach to the dropping position and a wild desire to escape the effects of this deathly hailstorm.

'And so we jink and swerve, an instinct of living guiding my legs and right arm; two large clear shapes on our starboard side are monstrous in the background of flares. We turn until the right hand battleship is between the bars of the torpedo sight, dropping down as we do so. The water is close beneath our wheels, so close I am wondering which is to happen first – the torpedo going or our hitting the sea – then we level out, and almost without thought the button is pressed and a jerk tells me that the 'fish' is gone.

'We are back close to the shore we started from, darting in and out of a rank of merchant ships for protection's sake. But our troubles are by no means over; for in our darting hither and thither we run slap into an 'Artigliere' class destroyer. We are on top of her fo'c's'le before I realise that she hasn't opened fire on us, and though I am ready for his starboard Pom-Pom, he has a sitting shot at something between 50 and 100yds. The white balls come scorching across our quarter as we turn and twist over the harbour; the cruisers have turned their fire on us again, making so close a pattern that I can smell the acrid smoke of their tracer. This is the end – we cannot get away with this maelstrom around us. Yet as a trapped animal will fight like fury for its life, so we redouble our efforts at evasion. I am thinking 'Either I can kill myself or they can kill me' and flying the machine close down on the water wing-tips all but scraping it at every turn, throttle full open and wide back.

'With a shock I realise that we are clear of the worst of it anyway. Ahead is the island that lies between the horns of the Outer Harbour, a low black mass that, at our speed of 120 knots, is suddenly upon us. We blithely sail by its western foot, oblivious of what it may contain, when comes the tearing sound of shell as red balls spurt from a position no more than a hundred yards away, passing close ahead of us. Away we turn to starboard, then, as the stream grows, round to port again, and so we zig-zag out into the open sea.... At last we are free to climb. At 3,000ft it is cool and peaceful, a few shining clouds casting their dark shadows on the sea and the warm orange cockpit light showing up the instruments that must tell me all is well. All we have to do now is to get back and land on, thoughts that worry me not at all.'[7]

After this brilliantly delivered attack, it is sad to have to record that his torpedo, alas, missed its target and exploded on hitting the ground on the *Littorio*'s starboard quarter at about 2315.

Meanwhile, the four bomb-armed Swordfish were carrying out their part in the attack. E5A, with Captain O. Patch, RM, as Pilot and Lieutenant D.G. Goodwin, RN, as Observer, arrived over San Pietro Island at 2306 at a height of 8,500ft (2,590m) and headed for the Mar Piccolo where his targets, the enemy cruisers and destroyers moored stern to the jetty, were lying. In the midst of the smoke and flame from the A/A gunfire which surrounded them, they were difficult to distinguish, but at last he saw them and dived to attack. When down to almost masthead height, Patch flattened out and let go his six bombs, then turned east. Unfortunately no hits were obtained, but as he made good his escape over the peaceful Italian countryside he noticed a large fire burning a mile and a half east of where the ships were moored.

Aircraft L4L, with Sub Lieutenant (A) W.C. Sarra, RN, as Pilot with Midshipman (A) J. Bowker, RN, as Observer, crossed the enemy coast to the west of Taranto at a height of 8,000ft (2,438m) and dived down to 1,500ft (457m) over the Mar Piccolo. Unable to pick out his target, he passed over the dockyard and suddenly spotted the hangars and slipways of the seaplane base right ahead. Appreciating that these would make an excellent secondary target, he came down to 500ft (152m) and released his bombs. A large explosion resulted and the hangars burst into flames. Belatedly the batteries and machine guns in the vicinity opened fire, but they did not prevent L4L from successfully disengaging to the south.

Aircraft L4H, with Sub Lieutenant (A) A.J. Forde, RN, as Pilot with Sub Lieutenant (A) A. Mardel-Ferreira, RNVR, as Observer, had lost contact with the main group and reached the area east of Cape San Vito just as Kigell, L4P, started to drop his flares. Forde arrived over the Mar Piccolo just as Sarra, L4L, was circling in search of his target. He picked out the ships lying stern to the jetty and looking like 'sardines in a tin' as he later described them. He let go his bombs from a height of 1,500ft (457m) but no hits were observed. Being uncertain whether or not his bombs had released, he went round and repeated the attack before breaking away to the north-west and crossing the coast five miles north of the harbour. Despite intense A/A fire from the enemy warships his aircraft was undamaged.

The last of the bombers, E5Q, with Lieutenant J.B Murray, RN, as Pilot and Sub Lieutenant (A) S.M. Paine, RN, as Observer, followed L4H to the east of Cape San Vito and on to the Mar Piccolo, bombing the line of ships and running across them on an east-west course at a height of 3,000ft (914m). One bomb hit the destroyer *Libeccio* but failed to explode. Murray then turned 180° to port and withdrew on the opposite course of the one on which he had approached. By 2335 the last aircraft of the first strike had withdrawn but the hornets' nest had been so stirred up that the guns continued to fire, putting up a barrage in all four sectors of the defence perimeter long after the sound of the departing aircraft had died away.

The Second Strike
At 1220 the *Illustrious* again turned head to wind and the second strike, led by Lieutenant Commander J.W. Hale, RN, of 819 Squadron with Lieutenant G.A. Carline, RN, as his Observer, began to take off. This time things did not go with the faultless precision of the first strike's launching. Seven of the nine aircraft had taken off successfully and the eighth, L5F, began to move towards the centre line of the flight deck when the ninth and last, L5Q, also began to taxi forward from the opposite side. The two aircraft met and their winds locked. Engines were cut while fitters and riggers rushed forward to disentangle them. L5F's

main plane had had some of its fabric torn off and several of the wing ribs were broken, but L5Q was undamaged. A consultation between Captain Boyd and Commander Robertson ensued and it was decided to allow L5Q to take off, but L5F would have to be struck down for repairs. By this time Hale had begun to wonder what had happened to his two missing aircraft; then a recount made the number eight and soon after a signal on a shaded lamp told him to 'Carry On' and so he knew that something had happened to L5F. It was now 2145.

The eight aircraft in 'V' formation had been flying east for twenty minutes when the straps holding the long range fuel tank to the fuselage of L5Q snapped. As a bomber and not a torpedo-carrying aircraft, the tank had been secured externally and not in the Observer's cockpit. Moments later it fell off into the sea, the engine cut and the aircraft rapidly lost height. By skilful airmanship Morford, the Pilot, nursed it round, restarted the engine and, although greeted with gunfire as he approached the carrier, he fired a recognition signal which caused it to cease and he landed safely.

By 2250 the sky had cleared and Hale took his formation up to operational height at 8,000ft (2,438m) and twenty minutes later he sighted the colourful pyramid of flak still being project skywards by the Taranto defences. His Observer, Carline, fixed his position from the feeble beam of the lighthouse on Cape Santa Maria di Luca on the eastern arm of the Gulf as they approached, keeping about fifteen miles off shore. The noise of their engines, picked up by the sensitive Italian airphonic listening posts, stirred the crews of the A/A batteries to even greater exertions, although the aircraft were not yet within range of their guns and the shells burst harmlessly in the air. At 2350 Hale turned north-east and five minutes later detached the two flare droppers, L5B with Lieutenant R.W.V. Hamilton, RN, as Pilot and Sub Lieutenant (A) J.R. Weeks, RN, as Observer, and L4F with Lieutenant (A) R.G. Skelton, RN, as Pilot and Sub Lieutenant (A) E.A. Perkins, RNVR, as Observer. The gunfire had momentarily subsided but, as these two aircraft skirted the eastern shore, it recommenced. Hamilton dropped his sixteen flares at fifteen second intervals and Skelton reinforced them with eight more. Then the two aircraft made for the oil storage depot, bombing it from different directions and starting a small fire, before they set course for a return to the carrier.

The five torpedo–armed aircraft were now skirting the northern shore of the harbour and were being subjected to the full fury of the gunfire aimed at them by the batteries ashore, supplemented by that of the ships themselves. Aircraft L5A (Hale) passing over Cape Rondinella at 5,000ft (1,524m) began to dive, jinking from side to side in an effort to avoid the hail of flak being directed towards it. The air was full of the reek of smoke from the enormous quantity of explosive which had been detonated during and after the first attack and it filled the throat and nose. Calmly, Hale selected the *Littorio* as his target and, when only 30ft (9.1m) above the water, he drove straight at her, releasing his torpedo at a range of 700yds (640m). He then banked steeply to starboard and, narrowly missing the cable of a barrage balloon, safely made his escape.

Aircraft E4H, with Lieutenant G.W. Bayley, RN, as Pilot and Lieutenant H.J Slaughter, RN, as Observer, followed the strike leader over Cape Rondinella, but its subsequent fate is not known as neither of the two officers was ever seen again. The Italian report of the action mentions an aircraft being shot down just west of the cruiser *Gorizia* and this may well have been the one.

Aircraft L5H, with Lieutenant (A) C.S.C. Lea, RN, as Pilot and Sub Lieutenant (A) P.D. Jones, RN, as Observer, also followed the strike leader's aircraft, but, finding the flak unpleasantly disturbing, turned a complete circle to starboard, and, losing height by this astute manoeuvre, got in beneath it. As he skimmed over the water on the northern shore he saw a Cavour class battleship beam on and released his torpedo at a range of about 800yds (732m). It struck the ship, *Caio Duilio*, on her starboard side abreast 'B' turret at a depth of 29½ft (9m). Narrowly missing the mast of a fishing boat, Lea took his aircraft between the cruisers *Zara* and *Fiume*, the guns of which were firing steadily at him, and then made good his escape over the northern tip of San Pietro Island.

Aircraft L5K, with Lieutenant F.M.A. Torrens-Spence, RN, as Pilot and Lieutenant A.W.F. Sutton, RN, as Observer, followed the other aircraft over Cape Rondinella and dived steeply through a veritable inferno of flak, aiming for a position five cables (914m) south of the Canal entrance. After he skilfully avoided a near collision with the unlucky E4H (Bayley and Slaughter), Torrens-Spence found himself in the midst of a confusing armada of ships, the guns of which seemed to be concentrating on his fragile 'stringbag'. Coolly selecting a Littorio as his target, he flew towards her and at 700yds (640m) he released his deadly load. While getting away, the aircraft's undercarriage hit the water, but with superb skill he guided it up between two barrage balloons and out across the harbour. However his ordeal was not yet over. Two floating batteries suddenly loomed up in the water ahead too late to be avoided. He jerked back the joystick, the aircraft rose abruptly and passed over them as the guns opened fire. They were so close that the airmen could feel the hot blast of the discharge, but by little short of a miracle, they escaped with only one bullet hole in the fuselage.

Aircraft E5H, with Lieutenant (A) J.W.G. Welham, RN, as Pilot and Lieutenant P. Humphreys, EGM, RN, as Observer, had chosen a route more to the north-east of Cape Rondinella. Passing over the Mar Piccolo and the town of Taranto, Welham turned to starboard, skirting the balloon barrage on the eastern shore. Up to that moment it seemed that his presence had not been observed, but suddenly heavy machine guns opened up on him and his outer aileron was hit causing him to lose control temporarily. When he regained it, he found himself in the middle of a square formed by four of the enemy's battleships and not in a good position to fire at any of them. Some very quick thinking was necessary and he decided to aim at one of the two Littorios. He launched his torpedo from 500yds (457m) on the *Vittorio Veneto*'s port quarter and, turning sharply to starboard, he made his getaway under an intense hail of fire. A 40mm shell hit the port wing and exploded, shattering some of the ribs and making a large rent in the fabric but Welham flew on and reached the *Illustrious* safely.

Aircraft L5F, which we last heard of being returned to the hangar for repairs after its unfortunate collision with L5Q just before take off, thanks to herculean efforts on the part of the fitters and riggers, had been made serviceable again in the incredibly short time of twenty minutes. As a result of eloquent pleading by the Pilot, Lieutenant E.W. Clifford, RN, and his Observer, Lieutenant G.R.M. Going, RN, Captain Boyd gave them permission to follow the remainder of their flight on their own. They took off 24 minutes after the others and made landfall five miles east of the harbour entrance. They had a grandstand view of the pyrotechnic display being put up for the benefit of their flight mates as they headed north-west over the town and dockyard. They could see from the oil streaked water and several fires that the enemy had taken a hard knock. The A/A barrage had died down and Clifford unhurriedly circled around looking for a suitable target to bomb. Dropping down to 2,500ft (762m) he dived across the line of ships and was greeted with a burst of fire. At 500ft (152m) he levelled off and aimed his six bombs at two cruisers, but no explosions resulted and he thought he had missed. In fact one of the semi armour piercing bombs had penetrated the thin plating of the cruiser *Trento* without exploding. Clifford then turned north, crossing the Mar Piccolo, before turning to starboard and out over the coast five miles east of the harbour entrance.

To Admiral Lyster and Captain Boyd the long wait for the return of the striking force was an agony of suspense. Although by no means a desperate venture, it was certainly a hazardous one, and the price exacted might well prove to be heavy. Promptly at 0100 the *Illustrious* reached the recovery position 'Y' and headed into the wind at 21 knots. The radar might be expected to give the first indications of the return of aircraft and, sure enough, at 0112 the operator began to notice one blip after another appearing on his screen. He passed the information to the bridge and in a moment the flight deck began to hum with activity as fitters and riggers tumbled out on deck and fire and crash parties assembled their gear.

The first to identify itself was aircraft L4C (Sparkle and Neale) which landed at 0120. The remainder of the first strike, minus their leader, followed at short intervals, Robertson carefully counting the score. Last to land were Patch and Goodwin in E5A, the navigation lights of which had failed, but they touched down successfully at 0155. It seemed almost unbelievable that only one of the twelve aircraft had been lost. No one knew what had befallen L4A (Williamson and Scarlett) but it was sincerely hoped that they had been picked up. Quickly the deck was cleared for the second strike, only just over an hour behind the first one, but at 0155, just as Patch and Goodwin touched down, Hale and Carline in L5A sighted the carrier and landed five minutes later, to be followed seconds later by Skelton and Perkins in L4F. Fifty minutes later Clifford and Going in L5F, the last of the second strike, touched down. Again the count showed only one aircraft, E4H (Bayley and Slaughter), to be missing. Considering the strength of the defences, the casualties were far less than anyone had dared to expect. Moreover, from the modest reports of the aircrews, it was difficult at first to discover the extent of the success which had, in fact, been achieved.

Chapter 5

Taranto Night and Its Aftermath

—⚅—

To Commander Bragadin on duty in the Operations Room of the Supermarina, it had indeed been a night to remember. As the dramatic events unfolded, 'news began to arrive by telephone from Taranto' he has recorded, 'news that grew more serious and surprising.'[8] When Admiral Cavagnari was alerted he went down to the Operations Room to see for himself what was happening. A stream of messages poured in and it was quickly evident that this was not a hit and run raid but a determined attempt to cripple his fleet. At first it was not possible to gauge the magnitude of the disaster beyond that at least three of the battleships had been torpedoed and that other damage had been inflicted on smaller ships and installations. All this had been done in spite of the anti-torpedo nets, the barrage balloons and the A/A batteries.

At Taranto itself, there was stupefaction at the blow which had been delivered. As damage control parties attempted to deal with the flooding in the stricken ships and others were fighting fires, Admiral Riccardi and his staff were busy mobilising all the salvage resources of the dockyard and despatching tugs and repair parties to those ships in need of assistance. Despite urgent requests from Supermarina for a detailed report of the damage, this was not forthcoming until the following morning and when it did, it was not pleasant reading. The battleship *Littorio* had sustained three torpedo hits, two of them during the first attack, of which the one on the starboard bow had blown a hole 49ftx32ft (15mx9¾m) in the bulge abreast Number one 6in (152mm) gun turret. The other, on the port quarter abreast the tiller flat, had made a hole 23ftx5ft (7mx1½m). During the second attack a third torpedo struck low down on the starboard side, just forward of the first hit, blowing a hole 40ftx30ft (12mx9m) in the bottom plating. A dent on the starboard quarter might, it was thought, have been made by another torpedo which failed to explode and which was subsequently found embedded in the mud beneath her. The ship was badly down by the bows and the forecastle partly awash. She would be out of action for a considerable time.

The battleship *Caio Duilio* had received one torpedo hit low down on the starboard side abreast of Number one 5.25in (133mm) gun mounting. It had blown a hole 36x23ft (11mx7m) between numbers 1 and 2 magazines which, as a result, were completely flooded and she had had to be beached. Most serious was the damage done to the battleship *Conte di Cavour*. She had been hit on the port bow under the foremost turret during the first attack. The torpedo had blown a hole in the ship's side measuring 40ftx27ft (12mx8¼m) and, as a result, numbers one and two oil fuel tanks were flooded and so were the adjacent compartments. She had been towed towards the shore during the night and abandoned at 0545/12 after which she had quietly settled. By 0800 almost the whole of her upper deck was submerged including the after turret. The Italian casualties had been comparatively light, amounting to 23 men killed on board the *Littorio*, 16 in the *Conte di Cavour* and one in the *Caio Duilio*.

When daylight came, the Mar Grande presented a distressing sight with its surface covered by a film of oil. The *Littorio* was surrounded by salvage vessels as strenuous efforts were made to save her. A submarine had been brought alongside to provide electrical power and a tanker on her port quarter was receiving oil fuel as it was pumped out of her tanks to counteract the flooding.

The Mar Piccolo, too was covered in oil which had leaked from the damaged tanks of the cruiser *Trento*. Although the bomb which struck her had failed to explode, she had a large hole in her main deck, and bulkheads and ventilation trunking had been damaged by the blast. The destroyer *Libeccio* had a fractured bow as the result of a near miss and the hull of the destroyer *Pessagno* had been damaged from the same cause. Firemen were still pouring water on the smouldering ruins of the seaplane hangar. In his office Admiral Riccardi was presiding over a conference convened to reconstruct the events of the night and to draw up the report so anxiously awaited by Supermarina.

The destroyer *Fulmine* had been ordered to move at dawn from the

Mar Grande to the Mar Piccolo, together with some other ships. She had on board Lieutenant Commander Williamson, RN, and Lieutenant Scarlett, RN, whose aircraft, L4A, had been shot down and crashed into the harbour during the first attack. They had managed to extricate themselves from the sinking Swordfish and to swim to a floating dock about 150yds (137m) from where they had surfaced. They were rescued by dockyard workers, who gave them a rough time, but took them to the *Fulmine*, where they were well cared for until taken ashore after the ship had shifted berth. They were eventually transferred to a Prisoner-of-War camp at Sulmona, but, following Italy's surrender in 1943, they were moved to Germany where they spent the rest of the war. Of the crew of the other Swordfish lost during the attack, E4H, the body of the Pilot Lieutenant G.W. Bayley, RN, was recovered and buried with full military honours in the cemetery at Taranto, but subsequently moved to the Imperial War Graves Commission's cemetery at Bari. Lieutenant Slaughter's body was never found.

However, apart from the crippling effect of the raid, what worried the Italian High Command was how a British carrier or carriers had managed to approach to within striking distance of the main naval base without being detected by air reconnaissance. As Commander Bragadin remarks: 'At Supermarina it was taken for granted that if British forces should come within 180 miles operating range of their torpedo planes from Taranto, the Italian forces would sortie to engage the British and prevent them launching an air attack on the harbour,'[9] but he does not explain why they were not sighted. To understand the reason, it is necessary to go back to the operations which preceded the execution of Operation 'Judgement'. On almost every occasion when Italian reconnaissance aircraft endeavoured to shadow Admiral Cunningham's fleet, they were either shot down or chased away by the Fulmar fighters flown off the *Illustrious*. On 8 November a reconnaissance aircraft had been shot down and seven S.79 bombers, which tried to get into position to attack, were turned back while still 35 miles away, one of them being shot down and another damaged. The following day, another reconnaissance aircraft was destroyed and yet another on 10 November, and a bomber formation broken up as well. In fact local air superiority over the fleet was obtained and this was a vital factor in the success of the whole operation. Describing the events, Admiral Cunningham remarks: 'The Fulmars were again very busy drawing off and shooting down shadowers with complete success. One of the most important requirements of the plan was unobserved approach to the flying off position.'[10]

The failure of their air reconnaissance was not lost on the Italian High Command as Commander Bragadin remarks 'The events of the night of 12 November, added to many other lessons, confirmed in the most obvious way the very critical deficiencies of Italian air reconnaissance. The fact was that large groups of enemy ships had been cruising the whole preceding day in the central Mediterranean and, at sundown, had crossed the Ionian and Adriatic Seas; yet the Italian reconnaissance had not given the slightest warning of their presence.'[11]

To Admiral Bernotti: 'The success of the air attack against the Italian fleet in the outer anchorage of Taranto was the first example of the formidable potentialities of torpedo aircraft against large ships in strongly defended bases and confirmed in general the capabilities of aircraft carriers.'[12] He went on to point out that the defences of the anchorage had been shown to be insufficient partly because the A/A defences were incomplete, but principally because the anti-torpedo nets were only 8m (26ft 3ins) deep, while the torpedoes were set to run at 10m (33ft). This was made possible by the employment of the Duplex pistols which came as a complete surprise to the Italians.

In addition to the attack on Taranto, the night had brought yet another blow. Force 'X', under Vice Admiral Pridham-Wippell, comprising the cruisers *Orion* (flagship), *Sydney*, *Ajax*, and the Tribal class destroyers *Nubian* and *Mohawk*, which it will be remembered had been detached during the afternoon of 11 November, proceeded at high speed towards the straits of Otranto. Its object was the interception of the Italian convoy which was known to run nightly across the Adriatic from Otranto, Brindisi and Bari. Passing south-west of the island of Corfu at 2030, Force 'X' steered to the north at 25 knots until 2230 when speed was reduced to 20 knots. The sea was calm, wind force 1, sky about 7/10ths clouded and the moon in the south-west, about three quarters full. On account of the bright moonlight, the Admiral kept his force concentrated and it escaped detection. It had sufficient time to reach the line between Brindisi and Valona, but not that between Bari and Durazzo, and there was only half an hour in which to deal with any ships sighted before the force would be obliged to withdraw in order to reach a prudent distance from the enemy air bases by daylight.

By 0100/12 Force 'X' had reached the northern limit and turned round when, at 0115, the destroyer *Mohawk* on the port bow of the *Orion*, sighted some darkened ships bearing 120° distant about 8 miles. They were an Italian convoy of four merchant ships escorted by the *Nicola Fabrizi*, a torpedo boat of 650 tons armed with four 4in (102mm) guns, accompanied by an auxiliary vessel, *Ramb III*, of 3,667 tons, en route for Brindisi. The *Mohawk* made the Alarm signal to her sister ship *Nubian* and closed the enemy at 25 knots. Selecting the torpedo boat as a target, she opened fire at 0125 at a range of 4,000yds (3,658m), hitting her with her fourth salvo. The enemy ship turned away making smoke.

The *Orion* had also sighted the enemy ships and altered course across the bows of the convoy, opening fire on the third ship with her eight 6in (152mm) guns at 0128, while simultaneously engaging the torpedo boat with her dual purpose 4in (102mm) guns at a range of about 6,400yds (5,852m). The merchant ship quickly burst into flames and one of two torpedoes aimed at her struck and she was seen to sink. The scene was now illuminated by starshell and *Orion* shifted her fire to the fourth ship, which was hit repeatedly and set on fire. After being abandoned by her crew she was torpedoed and sank by the stern,

The cruiser *Ajax*, which had sighted the convoy at 0125, engaged the torpedo boat five minutes later, but she passed astern and out of range, and so fire was shifted to one of the merchant ships, which was set ablaze. She then engaged the remaining one, which, being hit by two salvos, appeared to be sinking; a torpedo fired at her missed.

The cruiser *Sydney*, the last ship in the line, had sighted the convoy as early as 0121. She opened fire on the leading merchant ship, but after she was seen to be burning, the *Sydney* shifted her fire to the second one which appeared to turn away with shells bursting all around her. Next the hapless torpedo boat, now making smoke, came within range, but quickly drew too far ahead, and so fire was concentrated on the ships of the convoy now bunched together. The *Sydney* had a lucky escape when a torpedo passed under her at 0140. She was now firing at a merchant ship lying stopped and on fire and she fired two torpedoes at another one. The *Mohawk* and *Nubian* had also been busy. The former, after her brief action with the torpedo boat engaged the second merchant ship from the left, while the latter opened fire on a merchant ship at 0131 and when she was seen to be on fire, she shifted to another one.

At 0153 Admiral Pridham-Whippell broke off the action and

signalled his force to steer 166° at 28 knots. During the engagement he had received a report emanating from the British Naval Attache at Ankara to the effect that the Italian fleet intended to carry out a bombardment of the island of Corfu. As this could result in his being cut off by a stronger force than his own, and since the convoy and its escort appeared to have been destroyed, there was nothing to be gained by remaining any longer in the area. Although not known for certain at the time, the four merchant ships viz. *Catalani* (2,429 tons), *Capo Vado* (4,391 tons), *Premuda* (4,427 tons), and *Antonio Locatelli* (5,691 tons), all sank. The *Nicola Fabrizi* was severely damaged but managed to reach port, while the *Ramb III* escaped undamaged. In his official dispatch, Admiral Cunningham subsequently commented: 'The raid…was a boldly executed operation into narrow waters where the enemy might well have been expected to be encountered in force. It succeeded in doing considerable damage to the enemy and undoubtedly had considerable moral effect.' By noon on 12 November, Force 'X' had rejoined the Commander-in-Chief, who was cruising in a position between Greece and Sicily about 250 miles from the Italian coast.

On board the *Illustrious*, steaming at high speed to rejoin the Commander-in-Chief and the rest of the fleet, there was a natural feeling of elation, but it would not be possible to assess the results of the attack until air reconnaissance had obtained photographs of the harbour. The air crews themselves, in the pandemonium reigning over the anchorage during their attacks, did not have the opportunity to observe fully the results of their efforts. However, enough had been seen to leave no doubt that the operation had been a success. Just before 0700/12, as the carrier hove in sight, a two flag hoist fluttered to the flagship's mast head underneath *Illustrious*'s pennants, which was quickly translated into 'Manoeuvre Well Executed', the Royal Navy's traditional way for a Flag Officer to say 'Well Done'.

The fleet was still within range of the Italian air reconnaissance aircraft, so the *Illustrious*'s Fulmars at once resumed their task of shooting down the slow Cant 501 flying boats, which attempted to sight and report it. In the words of Admiral Cunningham: 'They (the Italians) did not have much luck, for three Cant flying boats were quickly shot down by the *Illustrious*'s fighters. The last air battle took place over the fleet and we saw the large bulk of the Cant dodging in and out of the clouds with three Fulmars diving in after her. There could only be one end, and presently a flaming meteor with a long trail of black smoke fell out of the sky and splashed into the sea just ahead of the fleet. One could not help feeling sorry for the Italian airmen who had undertaken such a hopeless task in their unwieldy aircraft.'[13]

Meanwhile, on board the *Illustrious* arrangements were going ahead to repeat the attack that evening, an action which the Commander-in-Chief had approved after receiving a signal from Lyster, in which he recommended that this should be done before the Italians had had time to strengthen their defences. However by 1600 Admiral Cunningham began to question the wisdom of demanding such further exertions from the carrier air crews. As one of them is reported to have remarked: 'After all, they only asked the Light Brigade to do it once,' but he left the decision to Lyster. The matter was settled by an unfavourable weather forecast at 1800 and an obvious deterioration in the weather in the area, which caused Admiral Cunningham to cancel the repeat operation and lead his fleet back to Alexandria, which was reached on 14 November.

The first information derived from photographs taken of Taranto by the invaluable Maryland aircraft was received on the evening of 14 November from the Vice Admiral Commanding, Malta, where they were based. It reported the scene as already described and ended with the words: 'Hearty congratulations on a great effort.' Captain Boyd, in his report, paid tribute to 'the excellent photographic reconnaissance promoted by the Royal Air Force' which was an important factor in the success of the operation. The decision to use Duplex pistols in the torpedo warheads he considered justified by the results, and he went on to mention that problem facing the *Eagle*'s air crews operating from a ship with which they had not had time to familiarise themselves. He referred to the problem of the contaminated petrol, subsequently traced to the tanker *Toneline*, which had led to the loss of three Swordfish. He praised the 'zeal and enthusiasm of everyone to carry out this great enterprise' and the skill of the pilots 'who, in these comparatively slow machines, made studied and accurate attacks in the midst of intense anti-aircraft fire.' Admiral Lyster deeply regretted the unavoidable absence of the carrier *Eagle*. In a private letter he expressed the opinion that her presence 'would have increased the weight of the attack considerably, and, I believe, would have made it devastating.'

Admiral Cunningham described the attack in his report as 'admirably planned and the determined manner in which it was carried out reflects the highest credit on all concerned.' Commenting on the entire Operation MB.8, he remarked: 'Apart from excellent results obtained in offensive action, perhaps the most surprising feature of the whole operation was the almost clockwork regularity with which the convoys ran, ships unloaded guns and material, and with which the rendezvous of widely dispersed units were reached at the appointed time.' At first the Admiralty was hesitant to believe the reports which reached it and which, due to transmission difficulties, were rather garbled when deciphered, but when the details were known, praise for those who had achieved such a success was unstinted. The Prime Minister, Mr Churchill, with a certain amount of understandable exaggeration, told an expectant House of Commons: 'The result affects decisively the balance of naval power in the Mediterranean and also carries with it reactions upon the naval situation in every quarter of the globe.' The First Lord of the Admiralty, Mr (later Viscount) A.V. Alexander, broadcast a glowing tribute to the Fleet Air Arm. *The Times* wrote: 'The congratulations and gratitude of the nation are due in their fullest measure to the Fleet Air Arm, who have won a great victory in the largest operation in which they have yet been engaged against enemy ships, and to Sir Andrew Cunningham who is the first Flag Officer to handle the new weapon on such a scale and has used it triumphantly.'[14]

On 18 November, H. M. King George VI sent Admiral Cunningham a message of congratulations in which he said: 'The recent successful operations of the Fleet under your command have been a source of pride and gratification to all at home. Please convey my warm congratulations to the Mediterranean Fleet and in particular to the Fleet Air Arm on their brilliant exploit against the Italian warships at Taranto.'

To the surprise of his Foreign Minister and son-in-law, Count Ciano, Mussolini did not take the news of the disaster which had overtaken his fleet too badly. 'A black day', Ciano recorded in his Diary, 'the British, without warning, have attacked the Italian fleet at anchor in Taranto and have sunk the dreadnought *Cavour* and seriously damaged the battleships *Littorio* and *Duilio*. These ships will remain out of the fight for many months. I thought I would find the Duce downhearted. Instead he took the blow quite well and does not at the moment seem to have fully realised its gravity.'[15]

Whether it was the attack on Taranto or the failure of Admiral

Campioni two weeks later to bring a much inferior British force under Admiral Somerville to action off Cape Spartivento, which caused subsequent changes in the Italian naval commands, is not certain. The British force included the carrier *Ark Royal* and doubtless this fact influenced the Italian Admiral's decision to avoid engagement. However, whatever the reason, on 8 December, Admiral Arturo Riccardi, formerly in charge of the base at Taranto, despite his lack of sea experience, relieved Admiral Domenico Cavagnari as Chief of Naval Staff, while Admiral Angelo Iachino, formerly commanding a squadron of 8in gun cruisers, relieved Admiral Inigo Campioni as Commander-in-Chief of the Fleet, the latter being nominated Deputy Chief of Staff.

Although three of Italy's six battleships had been put out of action overnight, none of them was damaged beyond repair. The *Littorio*, the moving of which was a somewhat delicate operation on account of an unexploded torpedo in the mud beneath her, was back in operation at the end of March 1941. Repairs to the *Duilio* were completed by the middle of May, but the *Cavour*, after temporary repairs 'in situ', was not refloated until July 1941 and was then towed to Trieste where work on her had not been completed when Italy signed the armistice in June 1943. The two undamaged battleships, *Vittorio Veneto* and *Giulio Cesare*, sailed the following day to Naples and later to La Spezia, where, at the end of January, they were joined by the *Andrea Doria* on completion of modernisation and working up. A division of 8in gun cruisers moved to Messina, but as Admiral Bernotti points out, this redistribution of the fleet was unacceptable as a permanent measure. 'By means of the aerial offensive' he wrote, 'the enemy had achieved results which obliged the nucleus of our naval power to move away from southern waters, that is from the area where they were most likely to be employed, bearing in mind the necessity of disputing the movements of British naval forces between the two basins of the Mediterranean.'[16] He goes on to lament the absence of any section of the air arm charged with the duty of fleet co-operation on a permanent basis. The enforced dispersal of the fleet in the Upper Tyrrhenian Sea appeared to him to emphasise more than ever the absence of air support and meanwhile, the enemy was able to move freely in any area in which his battle fleet wished to operate.

The Italian Admiral's remarks are more realistic than some of those made at the time by Churchill and other British commentators, who were still counting battleships as evidence of naval might, whereas it was the air situation which was to dominate strategy in the Mediterranean during the ensuing years of war. The fact that Admiral Cunningham no longer had to face a superior Italian battle fleet mattered far less than the attainment of air superiority. After the attack on Taranto, for a short while, he was in the fortunate position of being able to count on this, despite the superiority in numbers of the Regia Aeronautica. This happy state of affairs was short lived. The misfiring of the projected German invasion against England, coupled with the failure of the Italian offensive against Greece, prompted the German Naval Commander-in-Chief, Admiral Erich Raeder, to renew his pleas to Hitler to turn his attention to the Mediterranean, which was to have sinister results for the British forces.

Chapter 6

The Avengers

—⁓—

'The co-operation of the Axis powers in the Mediterranean might have produced decisive results for the general conduct of the war had it eventuated quickly and in a timely manner, immediately after the fall of France. Instead it was invoked to deal with a disastrous situation. Objectives which could have been realised relatively easily during the first months of hostilities became more difficult as the conflict progressed because Britain had the free use of the oceans.'[17] Thus Admiral Bernotti describes the situation as seen through Italian eyes as 1940 drew to a close.

On 20 November Hitler wrote his Axis partner a long letter putting forward a number of suggestions for remedying the situation in the Mediterranean. One of them was 'the transfer of German Air Forces to the Mediterranean mainly to act in co-operation with those of Italy against the British Fleet.' Later the Führer confirmed his intention to send an Air Corps to Italy for the purpose of weakening the British naval position, but he made it quite clear that he did not, as yet, contemplate sending German troops to bolster up the deteriorating Italian position in North Africa.

First elements of Fliegerkorps X, commanded by General Geisler, began to reach Italy in December and, by early January, 330 aircraft were deployed on the Sicilian airfields of Catania, Comiso, Trapani, Palermo and Reggio Calabria. They consisted of 150 Junkers 87B and 88 dive-bombers, 40 twin engine Messerschmidt 109 fighters, and 20 Dornier 18 and Arado 196 reconnaissance aircraft. All the pilots were highly experienced in operating over the sea and, in particular, in carrying out attacks against ships. The Italian Air Force could not boast of anything as formidable as the Junkers 87B (Stuka) dive-bombers, which had developed a deadly technique of getting high above their target and plummeting vertically downwards with an ear-splitting scream to release a 500kg bomb with great accuracy. Assistance to the Greeks in their struggle against the Italians was now one the primary tasks of the British Mediterranean fleet. In January 1941, it was decided to pass a military convoy through the Mediterranean from west to east under the code name of Operation 'Excess'. It included three ships loaded with stores for the Greek Army bound for Piraeus and one with stores for Malta. In accordance with a practice which had now become standard, Force 'H', under Admiral Sir James Somerville, would escort the ships as far as the narrow waters between Sicily and Tunisia; they would then continue with a small escort to be met by Admiral Cunningham's fleet to the east of the Narrows, and he would arrange for their onward passage. The Commander-in-Chief took advantage of the occasion to organise three subsidiary convoys, one comprising two ships from Alexandria to Malta (MW.5½), one of two fast ships from Malta to Alexandria (ME.5½) and one of six slow ships from Malta to Alexandria and Port Said (ME.6). The sailing of these was timed so that MW.5½ made the passage under cover of the fleet as it sailed west, while the other two were to leave Malta when the fleet turned east, the two fast ships joining Convoy 'Excess' while ME.6 followed a route further to the south.

The most dangerous part of the voyage, as always, was that through the Sicilian channel, where ships were exposed to attack from enemy air bases in Sardinia and Sicily and there was a likelihood of submarine and motor torpedo-boat attack, as well as the possibility of attacks by Italian surface ships. As an extra precaution, Admiral Cunningham told Admiral Somerville that he would send the cruisers *Gloucester* and *Southampton* ahead to join up with Force 'H' south of Sardinia to provide additional escort to the convoy after Force 'H' turned back. It then had to cover 150 miles before coming under the protection of his own fleet, which on this occasion, comprised the battleships *Warspite* (flagship) and *Valiant* and the carrier *Illustrious*, two modernised and one new ship, which he referred to as his 'First Eleven'. These would rendezvous with the convoy in a position 15 miles south-east of the island of Pantelleria.

The dispersal forced on the Italian fleet created a demand for a much greater reconnaissance effort on the part of the Royal Air Force units, based at Malta, which it was unable to meet and, in consequence, there was some anxiety in the minds of both Somerville and Cunningham, arising from an incomplete knowledge of the whereabouts of all the Italian surface ships. The several forces taking part in the Operation sailed according to plan and the enemy was soon aware that something was in the wind when Cunningham's fleet was sighted at sea soon after leaving Alexandria on 7 January. It was sighted again two days later, as were the cruisers *Gloucester* and *Southampton*, as they were about to join up with Force 'H'. A bombing attack by ten Italian Savoia 79 aircraft that afternoon on Force 'H' was unsuccessful and two were shot down by fighters from the carrier *Ark Royal*. During the night, after Force 'H' had turned back, an attack by two Italian motor torpedo-boats was repulsed with a loss to the enemy of one of them. At 0800/10 rendezvous was made as arranged with Admiral Cunningham's fleet and soon afterwards the first untoward incident occurred when the destroyer *Gallant* had her bows blown off by a mine. While she was being taken in tow, two Italian torpedo-carrying aircraft made an unsuccessful attack. At 1030 the fleet was sighted and reported by reconnaissance aircraft, but there was, as yet, no indication of the great change which had taken place in the enemy's striking power. At 1223 two more torpedo-carrying aircraft attacked from a height of 150ft (45.7m), dropping their torpedoes 2,500yds (2,286m) from the battleships, which had no difficulty in avoiding them. Unfortunately as it happened, four of *Illustrious*'s Fulmar fighters, on patrol over the fleet, spotted the intruders and swooping down, chased them until they were some twenty miles west of the fleet, claiming to have damaged them.

The three big ships were reforming after this curtain-raiser of an attack when a large formation of aircraft was reported approaching. The control in the *Illustrious* immediately recalled the fighters, ordering them to resume their overhead patrol, but two of them reported that they had used up all their ammunition and the other two had only a small amount left. So, at 1234, *Illustrious* altered course in to the wind (210°) and launched four more Fulmars and two Swordfish aircraft as reliefs for the fighter and anti-submarine patrols. While this manoeuvre was in progress, two loose and flexible formations of enemy aircraft were sighted and quickly identified as German Stuka dive-bombers as they took up a position astern of the fleet at a height of about 12,000ft (3,658m). The avengers had arrived. Singling out the *Illustrious* as their main target, at 1238 they began their attack. Sub-flights of three aircraft peeled off to make perfectly co-ordinated attacks, one from astern and one from each beam. Sometimes they dived straight from 12,000ft to release their bombs at about 1,500ft (457m), at other times they spiralled down to about 5,000ft (1,524m) before going into a dive and letting go their bombs, sometimes as low as 800ft (244m). Admiral Cunningham watched fascinated from the bridge of his flagship. 'There was no doubt we were watching complete experts,' he wrote. 'We could not but admire the skill and precision of it all. The attacks were pressed home to point blank range, and, as they pulled out of their dives, some of them were seen to fly along the flight deck of *Illustrious* below the level of her funnel.'[18] The carrier made drastic alterations of course in an effort to spoil the aim of her attackers but nothing short of two squadrons of fighters overhead to break up the enemy formations could have saved her.

At 1238 a 500kg bomb went through the loading platform of Number 1 Pom-Pom on the port side (n° 1 - see plan 3), damaging the gun and killing two of the crew, then passing through the gun platform, it bounced off the side armour into the sea and failed to explode. A second or two later, the first direct hit (2) occurred when a 500kg bomb landed right forward, passed through the recreation space on the port side and out through the flare of the bows to burst about ten feet (3m) above the water line. Damage from splinters was severe and there was some consequent flooding of the forward compartments. Next a 60kg anti-personnel bomb (3), after narrowly missing the island, scored a direct hit on Number 2 starboard Pom-Pom, killing most of the gun's crew. Damage to gun itself was slight, but ammunition in the loading trays caught fire. The jib of the mobile crane collapsed and jammed S1 Pom-Pom below and electric power to both guns was cut by splinter damage and blast.

Soon after, two bombs hit almost simultaneously; they were either two of 250kg or one 250kg and one 500kg. One (4) hit the lip of the after lift well at the starboard foremost corner, penetrated the lift and exploded on the floor of the lift well. The other (5) hit the light platform near the edge of the port side and exploded. The lift, at the time, was half-way between C hangar and the flight deck with a Fulmar fighter, in the cockpit of which the Pilot, a midshipman, was sitting. The combined effect of these two bomb hits was devastating. The aircraft disintegrated and the Pilot was never seen again; a number of Swordfish and four Fulmars in the hangar caught fire and, due to a combination of blast and fire, the ship was gutted between frames 162 and 166 right down as far as the armour over the steering compartment. All the electric leads in the area were severed by flying splinters and these included not only those supplying power to the after ammunition hoists but also those to the steering motors. To make matters worse a near miss (6) off the starboard quarter occurring at the same time, caused damage to the steering gear itself as a result of flooding. The ship went out of control and began turning circles with the rudder jammed to port. Lieutenant H.R.B. Janvrin (Observer in L4P) was climbing into his Swordfish to collect a first aid kit when he felt it being picked up and hurled sideways. The fire parties quickly went to work lowering the fire screens and dealing with the fires.

At 1242, a 500kg bomb (7) hit the flight deck one foot to port on the centre-line and half-way between the island and the after lift. It penetrated the armour and exploded beneath it about two feet above the hangar deck, in which it made a hole about 60ft square and set down the deck below it about four inches. This bomb caused considerable further damage. It buckled the forward lift into the shape of an arch, through which air rushed to fan the flames in C hangar and virtually blew out the after lift. The metal fire screens in the hangar were shredded and splinters from them wrought terrible execution amongst the fire parties and spray operators in the adjacent access lobbies. Fortunately the fire had not spread to B hangar, although it was affected by the blast from this hit. Damage was caused to the 4.5in gun ammunition hoists, one round exploding in the tray. Lieutenant H.R. M. Going (Observer in L5F), who had been watching the attack from the starboard catwalk hastened below to lend a hand. Finding that the officer in charge of the damage control party had been killed, he at once took charge and was assisted by other Pilots and Observers.

Further damage was caused by three near misses, one of which on the starboard quarter has been mentioned already. Another (8) on the port side caused a fire on the Senior Ratings mess deck and damaged lighting and power leads. A large splinter from this bomb penetrated the island structure and cut through the leads supplying the Radar, the Gyro compass repeaters and the 20in Signal Projectors. A third (9) near miss on the starboard side started a fire on the Royal Marines mess deck.

Amidst the bursting bombs, the flames and the smoke, the crashing of a shot down Ju 87 into the after lift well passed almost unnoticed, but its burning fuselage contributed to the holocaust caused by the bomb hits. Although the boiler and engine rooms were undamaged, the smoke and chemical fumes from the fires raging above them proved a serious hazard. These were being drawn in by the fans supplying air to the boilers and were essential for the combustion of the fuel, but they made the compartments well nigh untenable. Breathing through wet rags and drinking water from the auxiliary pumps to assuage their thirst, caused by the intense heat of the near red hot decks above them, the stokers gallantly stayed at their posts for almost two hours. Captain Boyd was to write: 'The courage and devotion to duty of the boiler room crew was magnificent.'

By 1303 the steam steering engine had been connected up and the ship was once more under control and at 1313 speed was increased to 26 knots. At 1330, when the *Illustrious* was ten miles north-east of the battleships and the latter were nearly the same distance to the south of the 'Excess' convoy, due to the high speed avoiding action which they had been obliged to take, a high level bombing attack by Italian aircraft, possibly assisted by some from Fliegerkorps X, took place. Seven aircraft attacked the two battleships, seven the *Illustrious* and three the convoy from a height of 14,000ft (4,267m), but no hits were scored.

From the reports which were reaching him, it was clear to Captain Boyd that his ship had been grievously hurt. Tongues of flame were shooting out of the after lift well and the interior of the after part of the ship was a blazing inferno. He decided to head for Malta at his best speed, an action in which Admiral Cunningham fully concurred and he detached two destroyers to accompany her, but at 1335 the steering gear broke down again and for the next hour the carrier made erratic progress toward her destination. However by 1448, steering by main engines, she was making good a course of 110° at a speed of 14 knots. Down below, under the direction of the ship's Executive Officer, Commander (later Captain) Gerald Tuck, RN, heroic efforts were being made to get the fires under control; then, at 1610 the enemy struck again. This time fifteen Junkers escorted by five fighters flew into position above the stricken ship, hoping to deliver a 'coup de grace', but thanks to warning received from the battle fleet's radar, they were met by the Fulmars which had refuelled and re-armed at Malta, and only nine of the enemy aircraft managed to get in their attack. By now, five of the six Pom-Pom guns and all four of the forward 4.5in gun turrets were back in action. The electrical supply to the four 4.5in gun turrets which had been severed by the bombs bursting in the after lift well could not be restored.

As before, the attacks were made from astern, from either quarter and from the starboard beam. Captain Boyd commented that 'this attack was neither so well synchronised or so determined as the previous one at 1240', but nevertheless one hit and one near miss did further damage and inflicted serious casualties. A bomb (10) believed to be of 500kg size landed in the after lift well where it exploded on hitting the after ammunition conveyor and killed or severely wounded everyone in the wardroom flat. All the officers snatching a hasty cup tea in the wardroom were wiped out and the whole of the after part of the ship was plunged into darkness. Many of the fire fighters were also killed but the blast blew out some of the fires. Lieutenant Going became a casualty, receiving injuries which necessitated the amputation of a leg. A few moments later, a near miss (11) close to the stern added to the flood damage in the steering compartment and killed everyone in the temporary sick bay which had been rigged up on the quarter deck. Another near miss (12) exploded in the sea, abreast of the island but inflicted only superficial splinter damage.

By 1631, the last of the enemy had disappeared, but the fight to get the fires under control continued and was not finally won until long after the ship berthed in Malta dockyard. At one time the flames were threatening one of the magazines and Captain Boyd was asked for permission to flood it. It was a difficult decision to make, but with the possibility of further attacks to come, he decided to take the risk, and he was fully justified, as, at 1920, when the smoking and battered ship was only five miles from the entrance to the Grand Harbour, the enemy made a final attempt to sink her. It was an hour after sunset and the moon was up when two torpedo bombers approached from seaward. They were met with a barrage of fire from the carrier and her two escorts which kept them at a safe distance, and the torpedoes, if dropped, were not seen, In charge of three tugs, the *Illustrious* passed St Elmo light on the breakwater at 2104, and at 2215 she made fast to Parlatorio wharf.

She had received, in all, seven hits, of which one failed to explode and another exploded outside the ship's structure, five near misses and one crashed aircraft. It was most fortunate that the bomb hits were not more evenly distributed along the flight deck and strange that the after lift well seemed to have such a fatal attraction for them. The four bombs which virtually wrecked the after part of the ship had all struck unarmoured surfaces, and the one bomb that did penetrate armour did so abaft the machinery spaces. Her watertight integrity was only affected by splinter holes. The damage to the steering gear caused a good deal of inconvenience but nothing more, and the damage control organisation functioned magnificently throughout the ordeal. Without the 'devotion to duty' of the boiler room personnel, the ship might well have been brought to a standstill at a critical time.

The bombing attacks, however, had taken a heavy toll of the carrier's gallant ship's company. Eighty-three officers and men had been killed, 60 seriously and 40 slightly wounded. Amongst the Taranto air crews who lost their lives were Lieutenant H. McI. Kemp, RN, Pilot of L4K, Lieutenant (A) R. G. Skelton, RN, and Sub Lieutenant (A) E. A. Parkins, RNVR, Pilot and Observer respectively of L4F, the former dying of wounds two days later. Lieutenant E. W. Clifford, RN, Pilot of L5F, Sub Lieutenant (A) A. Mardel-Ferreira, RNVR, Observer of L4H, Sub Lieutenant (A) A. L. O. Wray, RNVR, Observer of L4R, were also killed, the last named dying of wounds received. As previously mentioned, Lieutenant G. R. M. Going, RN, Observer of L5F, lost a leg as a result of his injuries, and Lieutenant (A) W. D. Morford, RN, was badly burned. However, a price had also been exacted from the enemy. The *Illustrious*'s Fulmar fighters added to the laurels they had already earned by shooting down some seven enemy aircraft, whilst the ship's guns claimed another six.

It was expected that the enemy would make desperate effort to complete the task he had failed to do whilst the *Illustrious* was at sea. The attacks, however, did not begin in force until 16 January when a raid by between 60 and 70 aircraft was mounted. They scored one hit, but the damage was not serious. Further heavy raids took place on the 18th and 19th, and, on the latter day, bombs bursting on the bottom of the harbour caused a mining effect which did serious damage to the main engines, fracturing the sliding feet of the port turbines and extensively damaging the piping and brickwork in the port boiler room. The ship's side below the armour was set in by five feet and the dishing extended over 75ft. That these attacks were not more successful was largely due to the fact that the fifteen Royal Air Force Hurricane fighters on the island had been reinforced by a further eighteen during the recent convoy operation and they, with the assistance of the *Illustrious*'s Fulmars, took a heavy toll of the attackers. Another fact which deserves mention was the way in which the Malta dockyard workers carried on with the essential repairs to the ship defying the danger from the air attacks. At last, 'by dint of superhuman efforts on the part of everyone' as Admiral Cunningham says, the *Illustrious* was made fit for sea and, at 1746 on the night of 23/24 January she slipped out of the Grand Harbour, unnoticed by the enemy, and, heading east at 24 knots, she reached Alexandria at 1330 on 25 January, where she was accorded a tremendous welcome by the assembled ships. After some further repairs, under the command of Captain Tuck (Captain Boyd had been promoted to Rear Admiral and appointed Rear Admiral, Mediterranean Aircraft Carriers, in place of Rear Admiral Lyster), she passed through the Suez Canal and, sailing around the Cape, safely reached Norfolk, Virginia, where she was completely refitted and repaired. She had fully justified the faith of those who designed the first armoured aircraft carrier.

PLAN 3

HMS ILLUSTRIOUS SHOWING BOMB HITS & NEAR MISSES ON JAN 10, 1941

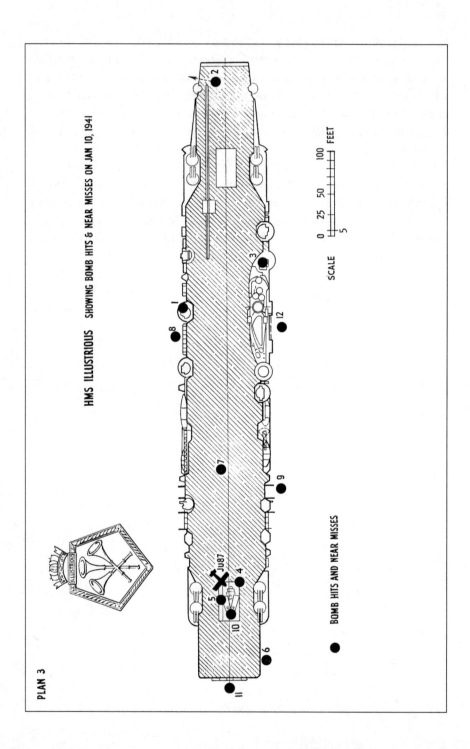

SCALE

FEET

0 25 50 100
5

● BOMB HITS AND NEAR MISSES

Epilogue

———∞∞———

As we have seen, Britain entered the Second World War with insufficient carrier strength and a belief that the gun was the final arbiter in naval action. Generally speaking, in the early stages of the war, carrier-borne fighter aircraft achieved little success in long range interceptions of enemy bomber formations attacking the fleet in northern waters. In fact, it was not until mid-1940 that the technique of fighter direction was successfully developed, first by HMS *Ark Royal*, the only modern carrier in the fleet at the time, and soon afterwards by the newly commissioned carrier HMS *Illustrious* during operations in the Mediterranean. The Skuas and Gladiators in service in 1939/40 had insufficient speed for attacking the German Junkers 87 and Heinkel III aircraft which were mainly used against ships, and when the Junkers 88 came into service the British aircraft were completely outclassed.

Italy's entry into the war further high-lighted the need for a good ship-borne fighter aircraft, since it became essential to provide cover for convoys passing though the Mediterranean with troops and supplies for Malta and the Middle East, especially in the narrow neck of water between Sicily and the North African coast, which earned the name of 'bomb alley'. Fortunately, at the same time as Italy's declaration of war, a new fighter, the Fulmar, became operational and , as has been relayed, reached the Mediterranean in HMS *Illustrious* in August 1940. Thanks to this new aircraft, to the use of radar and to a steadily improving standard of fighter direction, the Italian bombers and later torpedo armed aircraft, achieved comparatively little success. Most important of all, however, the arrival of the Fulmars created the conditions which made the attack on Taranto possible by preventing the Italian reconnaissance aircraft from shadowing the British fleet.

The successful attack on the Italian fleet at Taranto marked the beginning of a series of events which swept away the long cherished beliefs regarding the inferiority of carrier-borne aircraft compared with those operated from land. It confirmed the Japanese belief in the possibility of attacking the American fleet as it lay in Pearl Harbour and, ironically, it paved the way for the defeat of Japan by the seaborne air force of the United States Navy. Further, the surprisingly small number (eight) of carriers lost during the war, disposed of the bogey regarding the high vulnerability of these ships.

In the decades which have elapsed since World War II ended, carrier-borne aircraft remain an integral part of any maritime force operating outside the range of shore-based aircraft. This is particularly the case in the deployment of anti-submarine forces, since the helicopter is the submarine's greatest enemy. By the 1970s, the Soviet Navy, for so long reluctant to accept the need for carriers, was at last obliged to do so in its efforts to counter the activities of submarines deployed by the navies of the West. If we exclude the use of nuclear weapons, nothing has yet diminished the value of the carrier as a mobile, floating airfield.

PART II

Appendix I

Honours and Awards

—⚊—

After the praise so liberally bestowed on the personnel who took part in the attack on Taranto on 11 November 1940, it might have been expected that recognition of their gallantry would have been commensurate. However, the Supplement to the *London Gazette* of 20 December 1940 announced the award of the DSO to the Leaders of the two strikes, Lieutenant Commanders N.W. Williamson and J.W. Hale, RN, and of the DSC to their respective Observers, Lieutenants N.J. Scarlett and G.A. Carline, RN, as well as to Captain O. Patch, Royal Marines and his Observer Lieutenant D.G. Goodwin, RN, but that was all.

In the New Year Honours List of 1 January 1941, Rear Admiral A. L. St G. Lyster received a CB and Captains D.W. Boyd and R.M. Bridge, RN, of *Illustrious* and *Eagle*, were each awarded a CBE.

The meagreness of the awards caused considerable ill-feeling amongst the ship's company of the *Illustrious*, especially on account of the absence of recognition of the magnificent work done by the fitters and riggers in carrying out repairs after the disastrous fire, just before the attack was due to take place and ensuring that the aircraft were ready for service when required. Unfortunately by the time the attention of those in authority had been drawn to the matter, several of those whose names were to appear in a Supplementary List of Awards issued in May, had been killed during the air attack on the ship in January 1941. In this list, Lieutenant G.R.M. Going, RN, was awarded the DSO and Lieutenants F.M.A. Torrens-Spence, C.S.C. Lea, L.J. Kigell, R.W.V. Hamilton, H.R.B. Janvrin, A.W.F. Sutton, and Sub Lieutenants A.S.P. Macaulay, R.A. Bailey, P.D. Jones, A.L.O. Neale, and J.R. Weekes each received the DSC. Lieutenants H.I.A. Swayne, M.R. Maund, G.W. Bayley, H.J. Slaughter and Sub Lieutenants W.C. Sarra, and A.J. Forde, RN, together with eight members of the ship's company, were mentioned in Despatches.

Appendix II

Summary of Torpedoes fired during the Attack on the Italian Fleet at Taranto, 11/12 November 1940

—∞—

Target	First Strike	Second Strike	Total Fired	Hits
Littorio	1x365m 1x914m	1x640m 1x640m	4	3
Veneto	1x1,190m	1x457m	2	nil
Duilio	nil	1x732m	1	1
Cavour	3x640m	nil	3	1
Gorizia	nil	1	1	nil
TOTAL	6	5	11	5

Appendix III

Summary of Ammunition Expenditure
by Italian Shore Defences

—ɯ—

Cannon	125mm	1,430 rounds
	107mm	313 rounds
	88mm	6,854 rounds
Machine Gun	40mm	931 rounds
	20mm	2,635 rounds
	8mm	637 rounds
TOTAL		12,800 rounds

Ammunition expenditure by ships, the fire of which is limited to machined guns, is not known.

Appendix IV

Fleet Air Arm Personnel Taking Part
in the Attack on Taranto

—∽∞∾—

L relates to those planes dispatched from HMS *Illustrious*.
E relates to those planes dispatched from HMS *Eagle*.

First Strike

Aircraft & Squadron No	Name and Rank	Award
L4A 815	Lieutenant Commander N.W. Williamson, RN[1]	DSO
	Lieutenant N.J. Scarlett, RN[1]	DSC
L4C 815	Sub Lieutenant (A) P.D.J. Sparke, RN	DSC
	Sub Lieutenant (A) A.L.O. Neale, RN	DSC
L4H 815	Sub Lieutenant (A) A.J. Forde, RN	M
	Sub Lieutenant (A) Mardel Ferreira RNVR[2]	-
L4K 815	Lieutenant N. McI. Kemp, RN[2]	-
	Sub Lieutenant (A) R.A. Bailey, RN	DSC
L4L 815	Sub Lieutenant (A) W.C. Sarra, RN	M
	Midshipman (A) J. Bowker, RN	-
L4M 815	Lieutenant (A) H.I.A. Swayne, RN	M
	Sub Lieutenant (A) A.J. Buxall, RNVR	-
L4P 815	Lieutenant (A) L.J. Kigell, RN	DSC
	Lieutenant H. R.B. Janvrin, RN	DSC
L4R 815	Sub Lieutenant (A) A.S.D. Macaulay, RN	DSC
	Sub Lieutenant (A) A.L.O. Wray, RNVR[2]	-
L5B 813	Lieutenant (A) C.B. Lamb, RN	-
	Lieutenant K.G. Grieve, RN	-
E4F 813	Lieutenant M.R. Maund, RN	M

	Sub Lieutenant (A) W.A. Bull, RN	–
E5A 824	Captain O. Patch, RM	DSC
	Lieutenant D.G. Goodwin. RN	DSC
E5Q 824	Lieutenant (A) J.B. Murray, RN	–
	Sub Lieutenant (A) S.M. Paine, RN	–

Second Strike

Aircraft & Squadron No	Name and Rank	Award
L5A 819	Lieutenant Commander J.W. Hale, RN	DSO
	Lieutenant G.A. Carline, RN	DSC
L5B 819	Lieutenant R.W.V. Hamilton, RN	DSC
	Sub Lieutenant (A) J.R. Weekes, RN	DSC
L5H 819	Lieutenant (A) C.S.C. Lea, RN	DSC
	Sub Lieutenant (A) P.D. Jones, RN,	DSC
L5K 819	Lieutenant F.M.A. Torrens-Spence, RN	DSC
	Lieutenant A.F.W. Sutton, RN	DSC
L5F 819	Lieutenant E.W. Clifford, RN[2]	DSO
	Lieutenant G.R.M. Going, RN[3]	DSO
L5Q 819	Lieutenant (A) W.D. Morford, RN	–
	Sub Lieutenant (A) R.A.F. Green, RN	–
L4F 815	Lieutenant (A) R.G. Skelton, RN[2]	–
	Sub Lieutenant (A) E.A. Parkins, RNVR[2]	–
E4H 813	Lieutenant G.W. Bayley, RN[4]	M
	Lieutenant H.J. Slaughter, RN[4]	M
E5H 824	Lieutenant (A) J.W.G. Welham, RN	–
	Lieutenant P. Humphreys, EGM, RN	–

Notes

DSO Distinguished Service Order
DSC Distinguished Service Cross
M Mentioned in Despatches

Appendix V

Details of British Naval Aircraft

—ᶭᶭᶭ—

Fulmar
Two-seater carrier-borne fighter constructed by Fairey Aviation Co.
Power plant one 1,080hp Rolls-Royce Merlin VIII engine.

Dimensions	Span: 46ft 4½in (14.13m); Length: 40ft 3in (13.1m); Height: 14ft (4.26m); Wing area: 342sq ft (31.77m2); Weight loaded: 9,800lb (444.52kg)
Performance	Maximum speed: 240 knots; Rate of climb: 1,200ft/min (366m/min) Endurance at maximum speed: 2 hours Maximum endurance: 6 hours with extra tank at cruising speed Ceiling: 26,000ft (7,930m)
Armament	Eight fixed Browning 0.303in (7.7mm) guns wing mounted One 500lb (226.8kg) bomb

The Fulmars of No 806 squadron embarked in HMS *Illustrious* shot down ten Italian bombers between 2 September and 14 October 1940 and whilst giving cover to the forces engaged in the operations preceding the attack on Taranto, shot down a further six enemy aircraft. Described as 'a fine aircraft, manoeuvrable, with a good take off, moderate climb and plenty of endurance'[5] it was not however fast enough to catch the German Junkers 87 and 88.

Skua
Two-seater carrier-borne fighter and dive bomber constructed by the Blackburn Aircraft Company, Ltd.

Power plant one 905hp Bristol Perseus XII engine.

Dimensions   Span: 46ft 2in (14.5m); Length: 35ft 7in (10.8m); Height: 12ft 6in (3.8m); Wing area: 312sq ft (31m^2); Weight loaded: 8,228lbs (3,732kg)

Performance   Maximum speed: 196 knots at 6,500ft (1,981m)
Initial rate of climb: 1,580ft/min (481m/min)
Endurance: 4½ hours; Ceiling: 20,200ft (6,161m)

Armament   Four 0.303in Fixed front guns
One 0.303in Rear Lewis gun
One 500lb (226.8kg)

The Fleet Air Arm's first operational monoplane and dive bomber and the first to shoot down a German aircraft (Dornier No 18) during the Second World War. As a fighter it lacked speed and fire power.

Swordfish

Carrier-borne three-seater torpedo-spotter-reconnaissance aircraft constructed by Fairey Aviation Company Ltd. Crew of three carried for reconnaissance work and two for torpedo attack.

Power plant one 690hp Bristol Pegasus IIIM3 of 750hp Pegasus XXX engine.

Dimensions   Span: 45ft 6in (13.8m); Length: 36ft 4in (11m); Height: 12ft 10in (3.9m); Wing area: 607sq ft (56.3m^2) Weight loaded: 9,250lb (440kg)

Performance   Maximum speed: 125 knots at 4,750ft (1,447m)
Rate of climb: 10 minutes to 5,000ft (1,524m)
Range: 546 miles (7,16km) with a 1,610lb (730kg) torpedo
Ceiling: 10,700ft (3,261m)

Armament   One fixed synchronised Vickers gun forward and one Vickers or Lewis gun aft. Stowage for one 1,610lb (730kg) 18in (457mm) torpedo below fuselage or two 250lb (113½ kg) bombs below the wings, or one 500lb (227kg) bomb below the fuselage and one similar one under each wing.

The Swordfish was one of the most versatile and useful aircraft in the history of air warfare during the Second World War. It was generally known as the 'Stringbag'. Although outdated when the war began it remained operational throughout the war and proved its value in anti-submarine warfare many times over.

Appendix VI

Details of German and Italian Aircraft

—⁂—

Abbreviations

G   German
MP   Monoplane
BP   Biplane
F   Fighter
DB   Dive-bomber
I   Italian
TBR   Torpedo, bomber, and reconnaissance

Description	*Crew*	*Armament*	*Speed.Max/Cruising Range-Miles*	
G-*Me* 109 F.MP single engine	1	1x7.9mm 2x20mm	317/178	655
G-*Me* 110 F.MP twin engine	2	4x7.9mm 1x20mm	328/160	1,200
I-*CR* 42 F.Bp single engine	1	2x12.7mm	262/132	690
G-*Ju* 87D DB.MP single engine	2	2,000lb of bombs 4x2.79mm	204/159	670
G-*Ju* 88 TBR MP twin engine	4	5,000lb of bombs 5x7.9mm 1x20mm	249/180	1,900
G-*He* 111 TBR MP twin engine	5/6	7x7.9mm 2x20mm	218/166	1,930
G-*F.W* 200 TBR MP four engines	5/7	900lb of bombs 20mm turret 1x7.9mm	213/147	2,700

Description	Crew	Armament	Speed.Max/Cruising Range-Miles	
I-*S.79* MP three engines	4/5	2,500lb of bombs 3x12.7mm ½ 7.7mm	227/136	1,700
I-*Cant* 501 MP single engine flying boat	4/5	4.77mm	134/72	2,700

Appendix VII

Ship's Data (British)

—⚊—

HMS *Illustrious* – aircraft carrier

Captain Denis W. Boyd, DSC, *Royal Navy*

Displacement:	23,000 tons
Dimensions:	length 673ft (205m) pp 743ft 6½in (226m) overall (LOA) beam 95ft 9in (29.2m). Freeboard to top of flight deck 42ft 2in (13m)
Draught:	24ft (7.3m)
Propulsion:	Geared turbines, 3 shafts SHP 111,000 Oil fuel 4,640 tons
Speed:	30 knots
Protection:	Main belt 4½in (114mm) Hangar sides 4½in (114mm) Flight deck 2½-3in (63-76mm)
Armament:	Sixteen 4.5in (114mm) DP guns (8x2) 400 rounds per gun Forty-eight 2 pdr A/A guns (6x8) 1,800 rounds per barrel Eight 20mm A/A guns (8x1) Four 0.5in Machine guns
Aircraft:	36.24 Swordfish T.S.R. 815 and 819 squadrons, 12 Fighters (8 Skuas, 4 Fulmars) 806 squadron, Aircraft torpedoes 45, Petrol 50,000 gallons, One accelerator
Builders:	Vickers Armstrong, Barrow, Launched 5 April 1939, Commissioned 16 April 1940
Complement:	1,392

Remarks on HMS *Illustrious's* Protection

The expectation that British carriers would be required to operate in waters to which German and Italian shore-based aircraft would have easy access and which the Royal Air Force was not strong enough to dominate, was taken into account by the Admiralty when the design of the new carriers was considered in 1936. On the recommendation of the Controller of the Navy, Rear Admiral R. G. Henderson, it was decided to incorporate a considerable amount of armour protection at the expense of the number of aircraft, which could be carried. This proved to be a very sound decision and the final design, which was approved by the Board of Admiralty on 21 July 1936, reflects great credit on the Director of Naval Construction, Sir Stanley Goodall, and his staff.

The Illustrious class differed from the only post war built carrier HMS *Ark Royal*, by having a hangar which was virtually an armoured box within the hull. It was sited beneath a flight deck of 3in (76mm) armour, considered proof against a 500lb (227kg) bomb dropped from a height of less than 7,000ft (2,134m), or a 1,000lb (453.6kg) armour piercing bomb dropped from a height of less than 4,500ft (1,373m). The hangar sides and ends were mad of 4in (102mm) armour and the lifts, of which there were two on the centre line, one forward and one aft, were provided with armoured shutters. The main deck below the hangar deck was of 3in (76mm) armour and covered the machinery spaces, magazines and fuel stowage. The side armour which extended down from the level of the hangar deck to 5ft (1½m) below the standard water level, was 4½in (114.5mm) thick and covered 300ft (91m) of the midship section of the ship and known as the citadel. Where the belt ended a 2½in (63.5mm) transverse armoured bulkhead was fitted both forward and aft. The bulkheads of the steering gear compartment were also made of 2½in (63.5mm) armour and overhead a 3in (76mm) deck was fitted which extended forward to overlap the armoured flight deck above it.

The ship was fitted with anti-torpedo compartments inside the hull along the length of the citadel. These were designed to absorb the shock of the explosion of a 750lb torpedo warhead. The risk of a petrol fire was minimised by stowing aviation spirit in cylinders inside tanks filled with water.

Remarks on Radar
The *Illustrious* was fitted with Type 79 (Air Warning) radar only and her completion was delayed two months in order that it could be installed.

The Mediterranean fleet as a whole, after the arrival of reinforcements in August 1940, was quite well equipped in this respect. The battleship *Valiant,* the cruiser *Ajax*, and the A/A cruisers *Coventry* and *Calcutta* all had Type 79 or 279, while the cruisers *Berwick* and *Glasgow* both had Type 286, so that during operation MB.8 there were fifteen radar fitted ships at sea with the fleet.

Appendix VIII

Ship's Data (Italian)

—∿—

As a result of the Washington Treaty on the Limitation of Naval Armaments signed in 1922, Italy was entitled to begin capital ship construction up to a total of 70,000 tons in 1927. Instead, however, of availing itself of this opportunity to renew the battle fleet, the Italian Government decided to modernise thoroughly two of the four Cavour class, all of which had been completed during the First World War. Work did not begin until 1933 and was not completed until 1937. It involved a radical transformation of the interior of each ship which, with the exception of the hull, were virtually rebuilt and fitted with underwater protection against torpedo attack. New machinery was installed, resulting in an increase of speed to 27 knots. To compensate for the extra weight added, the main armament was reduced from thirteen guns to ten and new guns were fitted, the calibre being increased from 12in (305mm) to 12.6in (320mm) and, at the same time, a new mounting enabled the elevation to be increased to give a maximum range attainable of 36,000yds (32,918m). The secondary armament was replaced by more modern weapons and a new Conning Tower and Director Tower were fitted. So successful was the modernisation that it was decided to carry out similar alterations in the other two ships of the class, but work on these ships was not completed when hostilities began.

Battleships	Built by	Laid down	Launched	Completed
Conte di Cavour*	Arsenale di Spezia	10/8/10	10/8/11	1/4/15
Giulio Cesare*	Cantiere del Tirreno	23/6/10	29/11/13	
Andrea Doria +	Arsenale di Spezia	24/3/12	30/3/13	13/3/16
Caio Duilio++	Cantiere di Castellamare di Stabia	24/2/12	24/4/13	10/5/15

*Reconstructed between October 1933 and October 1937
+Reconstructed between April 1937 and October 1940
++Reconstructed between April 1937 and July 1940

Displacement:	28,700 tons standard
Dimensions:	Length 577ft (176m) Overall (LOA) Beam 92ft (28m)
Draught:	29½ft (8.9m)
Propulsion:	Parson's geared turbines on 2 shafts SHP 85,000
Speed:	Designed 22 knots, but after reconstruction 27 knots
Armament:	Ten 12.6in (320mm) 44 cal (3x2 and 2x2), Twelve 5.2in (133mm) *Cavour* & *Cesare* (6x2), Twelve 5.2in (133mm) *Doria* & *Duilio* (4x3), Eight 3.9in A/A (100mm) *Cesare* only (4x2), Ten 3.5in (88mm) A/A *Doria* & *Duilio* (5x2), 39 A/A Machine guns.
Protection:	Main belt 9¾in (250mm), belt ends 5in (127mm), deck 1.6in (40mm), Conning Tower 11in (280mm) *Cavour* & *Cesare*, 12½in (320mm) *Doria* & *Duilio*. Main turrets 9¾in (250mm). Secondary turrets 5in (127mm) *Cavour* & *Cesare*, 6in (152mm) *Doria* & *Duilio*.
Complement:	1,495 *Catapults:* 2 *Aircraft:* 4

Battleships	*Built by*	*Laid down*	*Launched*	*Completed*
Littorio	Ansaldo, Genoa	28/10/34	22/8/37	6/5/40
Vittorio Veneto	San Marco, Trieste	28/10/34	25/7/37	28/4/40

Displacement:	35,000 tons standard
Dimensions:	Length 774ft (235½m) Overall (LOA) Beam 106ft (32.3m)
Draught:	28ft (8.5m)
Propulsion:	Parsons Geared turbines on 4 shafts SHP 150,000
Speed:	30 knots
Armament:	Nine 15in (380mm) (3x3) 50 cal, Twelve 6in (152mm) (4 x3) 55 cal, Twelve 3.5in A/A (88mm) (6x2), 40 A/A Machine Guns 48 cal
Protection:	Main belt 12in (305mm), deck 5.9in (150mm)
Catapults:	2. *Aircraft:* 3.
Complement:	1,600

Note: In the design of these ships, special attention was paid to the vertical, horizontal, and under-water protection.

Notes

—⁊⁊⁊—

Chapters
1   Admiral Bernotti, *La Guerra sui Mari*, Tome I, pp. 166-8
2   Commander M. A. Bragadin, Italian Navy, *The Italian Navy in World War II*, p. 33.
3   Ibid.
4   Admiral of the Fleet Viscount Cunningham, KT, GCB, OM, DSO, *Sailor's Odyssey*, p. 267.
5   Bragadin, *The Italian Navy in World War II*, p. 44.
6   Ibid.
7   Excerpt from *A Taranto Diary* by Lieutenant M.R. Maund, DSC, RN, in *Flying Tales from Blackwoods*, Series 1.
8   Bragadin, *The Italian Navy in World War II*, p. 45.
9   Ibid. p. 46.
10 Cunningham, *Sailor's Odyssey*, p. 284.
11 Bragadin, *The Italy Navy in World War II*, p. 48.
12 Bernotti, *La Guerra sui Mari*, p. 221.
13 Cunningham, *Sailor's Odyssey*, p. 287.
14 *The Times*, 14 November 1940.
15 Ciano's Diary, ed. Malcolm Muggeridge.
16 Bernotti, *La Guerra Sui Mari*, p. 277.
17 Ibid. p. 240.
18 Cunningham, *Sailor's Odyssey*, p. 303.

Appendices
1 Taken prisoner.
2 Killed during subsequent bombing of HMS *Illustrious*.
3 Wounded during subsequent bombing of HMS *Illustrious*.
4 Did not return from attack.
5 British Naval Aircraft Since 1912 by Owen Thetford, Putnam & Co. 1971, p. 145.

Acknowledgements

—⁂—

The author wishes to thank all those who, in one way or another, assisted him with the writing of this book, particularly Rear-Admiral P.N. Buckley, CB, DSO, the staff of the Admiralty Library, Captain C.L. Keighley-Peach, DSO, OBE, RN, and Captain F.M. Torrens-Spence, DSO, DSC, RN, and Major General G.N.C. Galuppini, Head of the Ufficio Storico della Marina Militare Italiana.

The author and publishers wish to thank all those who gave permission for quotations to be made in this volume from the books of which they hold the copyright, viz. The United States Naval Institute, Messrs Hutchinson and E.P. Dutton for the Estate of the late Admiral of the Fleet, Viscount Cunningham of Hyndhope, Messrs William Blackwood and Sons, the Societa Editrice Tirrena, and the Keeper of Navy Records, The National Archives.

The illustrations reproduced are by the courtesy of the Imperial War Museum, and the Historical Branch of the Italian Navy.

B.B. Schofield, 1972.

Select Bibliography

—ᴍ—

Bernotti, Ammiraglio Designato d'Armata Romeo, *La Guerra Sui Mari Nel Conflitto Mondiale* 1939-1941, Vol. 1, Societa Editrice Tirrena, Livorno, 1947.

Bragadin, Commander Marc'Antonin, Italian Navy, *The Italian Navy in World War II*, United States Naval Institute, Annapolis, 1957.

Brassey's Annual 1959, Edited by Rear Admiral H. G. Thursfield, Wm Clowes Ltd.

Cameron, Ian, *Wings of the Morning: The British Fleet Air Arm in World War II*, Wm. Morrow and Co. 1963.

Ciano's Diary, 1939-43, Edited and with an Introduction by Malcolm Muggeridge, Wm Heinemann Ltd, 1947.

Cunningham of Hyndhope, Admiral of the Fleet Viscount, KT, GCB, OM, DSO, *A Sailor's Odyssey*, Hutchinson & Co., Ltd, 1951.

Kemp, Lieutenant Commander P. K., OBE, RN, *Fleet Air Arm*, Jenkins (Herbert) Ltd, 1954.

Illustrious, HMS, Ship's Log, The National Archives, accessed 1972.

Maund, Lieutenant M.R., DSC, RN, *A Taranto Diary* in *Flying Tales from Blackwoods*, Series 1,1957.

Moore, John, *The Fleet Air Arm: A Short Account of its History and Achievements*, Chapman and Hall Ltd, 1943.

Newton, Don, and Hampshire, A. Cecil, *Taranto*, Wm Kimber & Co Ltd, London, 1959.

Poolman, Kenneth, HMS *Illustrious*: *The Fight for Life*, Wm Kimber & Co Ltd, London, 1954.

Thetford, Owen, *British Naval Aircraft*, Putman & Co Ltd, 1971.

Warship Profiles Nos 10 and 11, HMS *Illustrious*, Profile Publications Ltd, Coburg House, Windsor, Berks.

Admiral of the Fleet Viscount Cunningham of Hyndhope KT, GCB, OM, DSO, Commander-in-Chief, Mediterranean 1939–41.

Vice Admiral Sir Lumley St G. Lyster KCB, CVO, CBE, DSO, Flag Officer (Air) Mediterranean, in conversation with Captain Ian Robertson RN.

Captain (later Admiral Sir) Denis Boyd KCB, CBE, DSC, Commanding Officer, HMS *Illustrious* (1940–41).

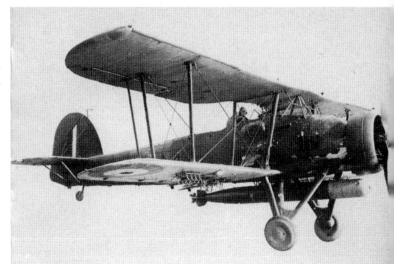

A Fairey Swordfish aircraft armed with an 18 inch torpedo.

A Glenn Martin Maryland reconnaissance aircraft used to take photographs of Taranto harbour before and after the attack.

The Italian battleship *Vittorio Veneto* damaged during the attack.

(*Top*) The Italian battleship *Andrea Doria* present in Taranto but undamaged.

(*Left*) The Italian battleship *Caio Duilio* with upper deck awash after the attack.

(*Bottom*) Photograph of Taranto harbour after the attack showing the damaged battleship *Caio Duilio* beached and listing to starboard.

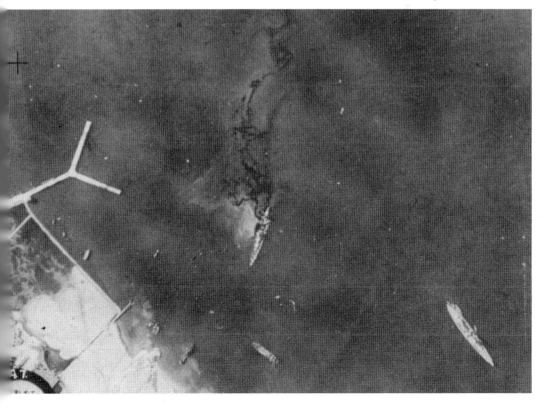

A near miss off
Illustrious's port bow.

Scene on *Illustrious*'s flight
deck looking aft during
the attack.

Scene during the attack
on *Illustrious* in Malta
harbour on 16 January
1941.

The *Bismarck* in a Norwegian Fiord, taken from the *Prinz Eugen*.

Admiral Lutjens inspecting the crew of the *Prinz Eugen*.

The mystery surrounding the whereabouts of the German battleship *Bismarck* was solved by this reconnaissance photograph taken by an aircraft of Coastal Command. It revealed her in Dobric Fiord just before she weighed anchor for her first and last sortie.

(*Top*) British Battle Cruiser HMS *Hood*. (*Bottom*) The *Bismarck* in action against the *Hood*. Photographs taken from the *Prinz Eugen* on 24 May 1941.

Aerial view of HMS *King George V*.

The *Bismarck* engaging HMS *Hood*. Photographs taken from the *Prinz Eugen* on 24 May 1941.

Shell from HMS *Hood* bursting near the *Bismarck*. Photograph taken from the *Prinz Eugen* on 24 May 1941.

Bismarck action – (*Top*) The *Bismarck* underway after being crippled. (*Middle*) *Bismarck* – an oily streak and an ominous sky. (*Bottom*) *Bismarck* on fire at the closing stages of the battle. Photographed by shadowing aircraft.

The Loss of the *Bismarck*
1941

Introduction

In 1867 an unknown Captain in the Royal Marine Artillery, John Charles Ready Colomb, published anonymously a small book entitled *The Protection of our Commerce and Distribution of Naval Forces considered*. Already at that time the need to import food to feed a growing population of 26 millions, and raw materials to supply a rapidly expanding industry, made it clear that Britain was very vulnerable to any interference with her sea communications, but it took a long time for this fact to be appreciated by those responsible for the country's defence. Colomb died in 1909, having spent his life in preaching what was ultimately proved to be a thoroughly sound naval strategy, but by and large his views were not given much attention. As events moved towards the outbreak of the First World War, interest was concentrated on the possible outcome of a clash between the battle fleets which Britain and Germany had been building in intense competition with each other during the previous decade. Yet when war came, it was the threat to her sea communications offered by the German U-boats which brought Britain to the brink of defeat.

In the inter-war years, treaties, pacts and negotiations were the order of the day and under the Geneva Convention, Britain sought to obtain immunity from submarine attack for her shipping on which she was now more than ever dependent, the population having reached 46 millions by 1931. Further, the use of indigenous coal was being extensively replaced by imported oil in industry, and, in the Royal Navy, wholly so. Fortunately, as the threat of another war with Germany loomed larger, the Admiralty, rightly suspecting that the Geneva Convention prohibiting attacks on merchant ships, without making provisions for the safety of their own crews, to which Germany had subscribed, would not be observed once hostilities began, made arrangements to institute convoys in the North Atlantic. It soon became apparent that the forces available were totally insufficient to provide protection on the scale required, but it was the agreed opinion that a lightly escorted convoy was better than independent sailing. This time there were no opposing battle fleets, and, from the outset, Germany concentrated her attacks on British sea communications, although her Navy too was lacking in the means to do so as effectively as it would have liked. Nevertheless, the best use was made of the forces available, and, by the end of 1939, after only four months of war, they had accounted for over ¾ million tons of shipping. The following year, 1940, which saw the Germany occupation of Norway and Denmark, followed soon after by that of Holland, Belgium and the greater part of France, the toll grew alarmingly to reach almost four million tons. But in the face of all these disasters, under Winston Churchill's forceful leadership, and with the generous help of the United States, Britain was striving to build up her ability to continue the war alone. In factories throughout the land, the highest priority was being given to war production, but the inescapable fact remained that, without a steady flow of raw materials, food, arms and equipment from North America and the Empire, all these efforts would be in vain. Germany now controlled the Atlantic coast of Europe from the North Cape to the Spanish frontier and this had greatly advantaged her in the conduct of the war against shipping, which her U-boats were waging in the Atlantic. These, with some help from long-range Focke-Wulf aircraft operating from ports and airfields in occupied France, were taking an increasing toll of British and Allied merchant vessels. Mr Churchill has recorded his anxiety at that time:

> 'How much would the U-boat warfare reduce our imports and shipping? Would it ever reach the point where our life would be destroyed? Here was no field for gestures or sensations, only the slow, cold drawing of lines on charts, which showed potential strangulation. Compared with this there was no value in brave armies ready to leap upon the invader, or in a good plan for desert warfare. The high and faithful spirit of the people counted for nought in this bleak domain. Either the food, supplies and arms from the New World and from the British Empire arrived across the oceans or they failed.'[1]

And there was good reason for the Prime Minister's uneasiness. At the end of January the German battle-cruisers *Scharnhorst* and *Gneisenau* had succeeded in breaking out into the Atlantic where they had sunk or captured twenty-two ships totalling 115,000 tons and, early in February, the heavy cruiser *Hipper*, on a second foray into the Atlantic, had sunk seven ships totalling 32,806 tons, out of a nineteen-ship homeward bound convoy from Sierra Leone. In the first three months of 1941 raiders accounted for 37 ships totalling 187,662 tons and this added to the toll taken by the U-boats and other causes accounted for almost one and a half million tons of shipping. These activities were placing an ever-increasing strain on the limited resources of the Royal Navy, because to locate a skilfully handled raider in the vastness of the oceans required, as had already been found, a large number of ships and aircraft, and the last named especially were in very short supply.

German Strength and Weakness

Grand Admiral Erich Raeder, Commander-in-Chief of the German Navy, was a man of great experience and determination. During World War I he had been Chief of Staff to Admiral Franz von Hipper, Commander of the First Scouting Group and Beatty's redoubtable opponent in the clash between the opposing battle-cruisers at the Battle of Jutland. During that war the German High Seas fleet had spent much of its time in harbour and afterwards there was a great deal of criticism to the effect that its offensive value had not been as fully exploited as it should have been. He was determined not to repeat the mistakes of his predecessors, Admirals von Pohl and Scheer, and from the outset had determined on an offensive policy, despite the inferiority of his fleet *vis-à-vis* that of the British, and so far it had met with considerable success. The damage inflicted on British shipping by the pocket battleships in the first months of the war, despite the unnecessary loss of the *Graf Spee*; the risks taken during the Norwegian campaign, which notwithstanding heavy losses had paid a handsome dividend; the success of the two battle-cruisers during their recent sortie into the Atlantic; all these encouraged him in the belief that, 'offence is still the best means of defence.' He knew too that if Britain's lifeline with North America and other overseas sources of supply could be severed, she would not be able to continue the war. He did not, however, yet possess an adequate number of submarines to bring this about, and the effect of the sorties by the pocket battleships, cruisers and battle-cruisers already mentioned had been to oblige the British to use their battleships as escorts to their North Atlantic convoys. This policy had prevented the German surface ships from attacking such convoys and therefore from sinking as many ships as they might otherwise have done, but at last he saw a way of achieving what he hoped might prove a decisive blow. The new battleship *Bismarck* was now operational, and he well knew that she was superior in every way to any similar class of ship in the British Navy. But for all what he calls, 'her unusually powerful fighting strength,' Raeder was worried by his inability to provide his ships with air cover and this he fully appreciated was 'a weak point in our armour' and one about which he could do nothing since the war having broken out earlier than he had been led to expect, he had not had time to complete the building of any carriers. However, for the reasons given above, he decided to ignore this weakness, but he could have wished that his opposite number, the Commander-in-Chief of the German Air Force, Reichsmarshal Herman Göring, would be more co-operative, for there was quite a lot that shore-based aircraft could do to make up for the lack of a naval air arm.

The *Bismarck*

The battleship *Bismarck* was the fourth ship to bear the name of the 'blood and iron' Chancellor who, paradoxically, though he had forged the unity of the German nation, had seen no need for it to possess a navy. Since her commissioning on 24 April 1940, she had been in the Baltic overcoming the teething troubles found in all new ships, and working her crew up to the highest pitch of efficiency. When, at the end of November 1938, Raeder had shown Hitler the designs of the two new powerful battleships, the keels of which had been laid two years previously, the latter had criticised them 'declaring that they were insufficiently gunned and too slow', but the Grand Admiral knew better. Officially stated to conform to the 1922 Washington Treaty limit of 35,000 tons, the *Bismarck* and her sister ship the *Tirpitz* had a maximum displacement of 50,900 tons and 52,600 tons respectively, a secret which had been very well kept. Great attention had been paid to their underwater protection which, in addition to bulkheads of unusual strength, comprised a large number of compartments or cells capable of absorbing water pressure and of allowing the upward venting of the force of an explosion. These anti-torpedo compartments were constructed of a special kind of steel of great toughness and elasticity, capable of being bent by the force of an explosion without cracking. They were sited immediately below the armoured belt and within the hull plating. As regards armour, a 12½in (32cm) belt of the best hardened Krupp Steel, 170m long, covered the vital parts of the ship and extended from 3m above to 2m below the water line; although not proof against a direct hit by a 15in (380mm) shell, it was believed that any engagement with a similarly armed ship would be fought at a range which ensure only a glancing impact, which such high quality steel would be able to withstand. The horizontal armour comprised an upper deck made from 2in (5cm) special steel designed to detonate the fuses of shell and bombs before they were able to penetrate to vital parts of the ship. Below this was a main deck covering four-fifths of the ship's length made from armour plate 4in (12cm) thick, with sloping sides 4¾in (12cm) thick, reaching down almost to the lower edge of the side armour. It was claimed, with some justification and borne out by subsequent events, that these ships were virtually unsinkable. Originally designed to be powered by diesel engines so as to give them a very long endurance, the need to accelerate their construction led to the substitution of high pressure Wagner type boilers feeding three sets of turbines driving three propellers to give a designed speed of 29 knots. On trials the *Bismarck* reached 30.8 knots. This then, was the ship upon which Raeder pinned his hopes.

The *Prinz Eugen*

The heavy cruiser *Prinz Eugen*, detailed to accompany the *Bismarck* on her sortie into the Atlantic, was a sister ship of the *Hipper* and the unlucky *Blücher*, sunk during the invasion of Norway. They were officially supposed to conform to the 10,000 tons limit for cruisers laid down under the 1922 Washington Treaty, but in fact their tonnage was nearly double that amount, being 18,500 tons at deep load. In speed and protection they outclassed the 8in gun cruisers in the British fleet. She was the first ship in the German Navy to bear the name, her immediate predecessor being the 20,000 ton battleship of the Austrian Navy in the First World War which in turn had been named after the French General François Eugene, Prince of Savoy, and ally of Churchill's ancestor, the Duke of Marlborough, at the Battle of Blenheim. In addition to a main armament of eight 8in (203mm) guns she carried twelve 4.1in (104mm) A/A guns and twelve torpedoes. She became known in the German Navy as 'the lucky ship.'

Operation Rheinübung (Rhine Exercise)

Raeder's plan to which the code name of Operation 'Rheinübung' was given, involved a simultaneous sortie into the Atlantic by the battleship *Bismarck* and the cruiser *Prinz Eugen* from the Baltic, and the battle-cruisers *Scharnhorst* and *Gneisenau* from Brest, to which port they had returned after their last sortie. The ships were to rendezvous at a prearranged position, and with this powerful force he was confident that any convoy encountered could be overwhelmed. A series of such disasters would, he was sure, lead to a suspension of sailings and moreover such a concentration would pose a very difficult problem for the British who might be obliged to withdraw their battleships from the Mediterranean to meet it, and thus facilitate the domination of that area by the Italian fleet. Arrangements had been made to support the ships with five tankers and two supply ships, and special reconnaissance would be provided by U-boats and disguised merchantmen. It was a bold, imaginative plan, typical of the man who made it, and might well have succeeded, but for a series of unforeseen incidents.

Originally timed to be put into operation during the new moon period at the end of April, the first setback occurred when it was discovered that there would be a delay in the completion of the *Scharnhorst*'s refit at Brest. Then, on 6 April an aircraft from Coastal Command of the Royal Air Force torpedoed the *Gneisenau* as she lay at anchor there, and five days later, after she had been moved into dry dock she was severely damaged during a raid on the port by aircraft from Bomber Command. Later, as a result of running over a ground mine laid by aircraft in the Baltic, the *Prinz Eugen* suffered damage to a coupling, necessitating a postponement to the latter part of May when the moon would again be new.

Raeder had selected to command the operation an Admiral in whom, he has recorded, he had the greatest confidence, the fifty-two year old Günther Lütjens who had served with distinction in Torpedo boats during the First World War. The outbreak of the Second World War found him in command of all destroyers and fast patrol boats. In March 1940, as temporary relief for Admiral Wilhelm Marschal who had gone sick, he commanded the battle-cruisers *Scharnhorst* and *Gneisenau* during the Norwegian campaign and in July he was confirmed in the appointment. He had recently returned from a successful foray with these ships into the Atlantic. He has been described as 'one of Germany's ablest officers since the First World War. Very deliberate and intelligent, level-headed in his judgement of situations and people; incorruptible in his views, unassuming and an engaging person when you knew him well; devoid of vanity and without overweening ambition. His dry humour made him well-liked amongst his comrades.'2

When Raeder informed Lütjens of his decision to mount the

operation the latter pointed out that it would be far more effective if it were postponed until either the battle-cruisers or the *Tirpitz* were ready for sea. He also suggested that the appearance of the *Bismarck* in the Atlantic would cause the British Admiralty to take measures which would jeopardise the chances of success for an operation in strength at a later date with the other ships. While fully agreeing with him on this point, Raeder was obviously not prepared to change his views, for he went on to caution him about using Brest for the shortest possible time and only to replenish with ammunition or because of heavy damage. He ended, 'It is advisable to operate with caution. It is wrong to play for high stakes for a limited, possibly uncertain success. Our aim must be to carry out continuous operations with the *Bismarck* and later with the *Tirpitz* as well. To seek out a fight is not an end in itself, but only a means towards achieving the object which is to sink enemy tonnage. As long as this can be achieved without high stakes, so much the better.'[3] In his book Raeder says he was concerned at 'the gradual improvement of the enemy's countermeasures and in particular at the strengthening of his air reconnaissance system.'[4]

So all things considered, he decided that the operation must be carried out by the *Bismarck* and *Prinz Eugen* alone, as soon as repairs to the last-named were completed. The date finally selected was 18 May.

It was a comparatively minor operation for the Commander-in-Chief of the sea-going forces to command in person, a point of view which Admiral Conrad Patzig put to Lütjens when they were discussing the operation a week before it was due to begin, but while agreeing, Lütjens had no desire to query Raeder's decision though he appears to have had some premonition of the outcome, for he ended the interview by saying: 'I shall have to sacrifice myself sooner or later. I have renounced my private life and I am determined to execute the task which has been entrusted to me in an honourable manner.'[5]

Although there is no record in the Führer Naval Conferences that Hitler's approval was sought to the launching of operation 'Rheinübung' and Raeder says categorically: 'The responsibility for sending out the *Bismarck* was mine',[6] we have it on the authority of Captain (later Admiral) Puttkamer, Hitler's adjutant, that at the eleventh hour the Führer attempted to intervene. While the *Bismarck* was at Gotthafen, she was visited by Hitler, but Raeder being absent, the question of her employment was not discussed. It was not until the Grand Admiral appeared at the Berghof on 22 May and mentioned, almost casually, that the ships had sailed, that Hitler enquired what they were doing. On being told he 'expressed lively misgivings' and wanted them to be recalled. He was worried about the reactions of the United States, the possible complications with the launching of Operation Barbarossa (the invasion of Russia planned to begin on 1 June), and finally the risks of attacks on them by British aircraft carriers. Only after considerable discussion did Hitler agree to their proceeding as planned.[7]

PART I

Chapter 1

Moves and Countermoves

—⚓—

The Commander-in-Chief of the British Home Fleet based on Scapa Flow was Admiral Sir John C. Tovey, fifty-six years old but looking hardly a day over forty. He was a destroyer man, having spent most of his career in command of those fast moving ships in which quick thinking is essential. As Captain of the destroyer HMS *Onslow* at the Battle of Jutland, he had shown a good measure of the offensive spirit and initiative when, single-handed, he attacked the powerful German battle-cruiser squadron, gave the cruiser *Wiesbaden* her coup de grace, and successfully brought his badly damaged ship back to port, feats which earned him a well merited DSO. He was to display these characteristics of firmness of purpose and nimbleness of mind during the next few critical days. The main task of the Home Fleet at that time was to prevent a sortie by German warships into the Atlantic from ports in German and German occupied Norway. The successful escape of the battle-cruisers *Scharnhorst* and *Gneisenau* during the long, dark winter nights and their subsequent arrival at Brest had, so to speak, turned its flank and, in consequence, the Royal Air Force was obliged to make them a high priority target, an excellent example of the interrelation of the Services. It was known that the new battleship *Bismarck* must by now be ready for sea, and it was of the greatest import to prevent her from joining forces with the other two ships and providing a threat to shipping in the Atlantic which, in the circumstances, it would be very difficult for the Home Fleet to counter. The days when a British fleet kept ceaseless watch against a sortie of the French fleet from that same port were a thing of the past; with the threat of air and submarine attack ships could no longer exercise close blockade, nor could they lie in anchorages such as Torbay or Plymouth Sound waiting for news that the enemy had put to sea.

The Home Fleet relied largely on air reconnaissance, backed by intelligence, for indications of the movements of enemy ships. When news of the possibility of such moves was received, steps were taken to increase the amount of air reconnaissance and to back it up by surface ship patrols both in the 200 miles wide Denmark Straits between Iceland and Greenland, and also in the Iceland-Faroes passage. The former was the escape route most favoured by the German ships. It was narrowed by an icefield off the Greenland coast to between 80 and 60 miles, depending on the time of year, and a British minefield laid in a north-westerly direction and extending some 50 miles from the north-west tip of Iceland, of which the Germans were well aware, restricted the navigable water to between 10 and 30 miles. But, despite the utmost vigilance, bad weather and the long winter nights gave the enemy a reasonable chance of making the passage unobserved, especially as Coastal Command had insufficient aircraft in the early stages of the war to meet all the demands made on it. As already mentioned, the *Scharnhorst* and *Gneisenau* had successfully evaded interception when they slipped out into the Atlantic in January and so had the *Hipper* when she returned to Germany in March. Now, however, in May the shorter nights and hopes of less stormy weather favoured the British forces.

At the time when the *Bismarck* and the *Prinz Eugen* were preparing to set sail on their Atlantic foray, the Home Fleet comprised the two new battleships *King George V* (flagship of Admiral Tovey), and *Prince of Wales*; the battle-cruiser *Hood* (flagship of Vice Admiral L.E. Holland), the 8in gun cruisers *Norfolk* (flagship of Rear Admiral W.F. Wake-Walker) and *Suffolk*; the 6in gun cruisers *Galatea* (flagship of Rear Admiral A.T.B. Curteis); *Aurora*, *Arethusa*, *Kenya*, *Hermione*, *Neptune*, *Birmingham* and *Manchester*, together with twelve destroyers (see Appendix I). With the exception of the *Norfolk* on patrol in the Denmark Straits, the *Suffolk* refuelling at Hvalfiord (Iceland), the *Birmingham* and *Manchester* patrolling the Iceland-Faroes passage, the *Arethusa* on passage to Iceland with the Vice Admiral, Orkneys and Shetlands, the *Hermione* returning to Scapa after repairs to one of her turrets, and the destroyers *Inglefield* and *Intrepid* rejoining from the south, the rest of the fleet was lying in Scapa Flow. On paper, it would seem that Admiral Tovey disposed of an overwhelmingly superior force to that which the Germans could muster, but, as already mentioned, a ship – even as large as the *Bismarck* – is a very small object compared with the immensity of the ocean, hence to carry out a search a large number of them are needed and moreover they must either have the speed to keep out of range or be grouped in sufficient strength to deal with an opponent when located. In the circumstances with which this history is concerned, the last point is of special significance. The *Bismarck* being superior to any ship in the British fleet, a concentration of at least two heavy ships was needed to deal with her and this Admiral Tovey had to take into account when making his dispositions.

Comparison of *Bismarck* with King George V Class and the *Hood*
Although the ten 14in guns with which the King George V class battleships were armed, fired a broadside 220lb heavier than that of the eight 15in guns of the *Bismarck*, the latter was some 6,700 tons larger and structurally better built. Moreover, the *Prince of Wales* had joined the fleet as a new ship only two months earlier and was still having considerable trouble with her 14in gun turrets, so much so that the contractor's men were still onboard. As for the *Hood*, for twenty years the pride of the Royal Navy, although theoretically three knots faster than the *Bismarck*, she was now only capable of 29½ knots. Though her main armament was similar to that of the German ship and her main armoured belt was only half an inch thinner, it was not made of such tough steel, nor did it cover such a large area of the ship. In theory the main belt in neither ship was proof against a direct hit by a 15in shell. But where the *Bismarck* scored was in her horizontal protection already described. With all the additional equipment installed in the *Hood* since the outbreak of war, she was drawing three feet more than originally intended, thereby increasing her deep load displacement from 45,200 tons to 48,300 tons. A programme aimed at improving her horizontal and vertical protection had been drawn up but never implemented. She was in fact an old ship about to do battle with a brand new one.

First Reports of the German Ships
The first news of the sailing of the German ships was received on 20 May from the British Naval Attaché in Stockholm, after they had been sighted, but not identified, by the Swedish cruiser *Gotland* while exercising in the Skagerrak. When the information reached the Admiralty and Admiral Tovey, both acted on the assumption that the

Bismarck was one of the two ships sighted. Intensive German air activity in the area between Jan Mayen Island and Greenland, and frequent reconnaissance flights over Scapa Flow during the previous ten days had indicated that something was afoot, hence the cruiser patrols established in the channels to the east and west of Iceland. Appropriate dispositions were now made to ensure the interception of the enemy ships should they be about to break out into the Atlantic. The Admiralty arranged for Coastal Command of the Royal Air Force to increase air reconnaissance in the Shetlands-Norway area to a maximum and placed the carrier *Victorious* and the battle-cruiser *Repulse* at the disposal of the Commander-in-Chief, Home Fleet. The *Victorious* intended as part of the escort of troop convoy WS.8B bound for Gibraltar and the Middle East, was at Scapa embarking her aircraft. She, like the *Prince of Wales*, was a new ship and not fully operational. The twenty-five year-old *Repulse*, also part of the convoy's escort was in the Clyde. For his part, Admiral Tovey warned the *Suffolk* to be ready to reinforce the *Norfolk* in the Denmark Straits, ordered the *Birmingham* and *Manchester* to refuel at Skaalfiord and resume patrol immediately afterwards, the *Arethusa* to remain at Hvalfiord at the disposal of Rear Admiral W.F. Wake-Walker, commanding the First Cruiser Squadron with his flag in the *Norfolk*. He sent for the Captain of the *Victorious*, Captain H.C. Bovell RN and asked him about the state of his ship. He was told that she had 48 crated Hurricane aircraft onboard for delivery in Egypt, and that in consequence her complement of aircraft had been reduced to nine Fairey Swordfish torpedo/reconnaissance aircraft and six Fulmar fighters. Admiral Tovey says in his despatch that he would have liked to replace these last by 828 squadron of Albacores, which he had sent to Sumburgh in the Shetlands with a view to attacking the enemy ships in the vicinity of Bergen, but when it became known that the enemy had sailed, it was too late to do so. After discussion with Captain Bovell and his air staff officers, he decided that although the ship was not properly worked up, she was too great an asset to be left behind.

At 1315 on 21 May, a reconnaissance aircraft of Coastal Command reconnoitring the south-western coast of Norway, sighted two German warships at anchor in Korsfiord, a few miles south of the port of Bergen. Although the pilot cautiously reported them as two Hipper class cruisers, after the photographs taken of them had been examined there was no doubt that one of them was the *Bismarck*. Admiral Tovey was informed of this immediately and he ordered Vice Admiral L.E. Holland in his flagship HMS *Hood* to take the battleship *Prince of Wales* under his orders and with an escort of six destroyers (*Electra, Echo, Anthony, Icarus, Achates* and *Antelope*) to leave Scapa and proceed to Hvalfiord, Iceland, so as to be in a position to support the cruisers patrolling the straits on either side of Iceland. The ships sailed at midnight. At dawn the next day, six Whitley and six Hudson aircraft of Coastal Command attacked the German ships as they lay at anchor. The weather conditions were bad and the visibility poor, so that only two aircraft reached the fjord, and they dropped their loads of armour-piercing bombs on the off-chance of a hit, but without success.

Throughout the day, despite steadily deteriorating weather conditions, reconnaissance was maintained off the Norwegian coast and in order to do so, every available aircraft in the north-east area was pressed into service. The visibility, however, was so poor that they were unable to see whether the ships were still in the fiord or not. An attempt made that night by eighteen aircraft of the Royal Air Force Bomber Command to attack the German ships also failed; the coast was shrouded in fog and only two aircraft succeeded in reaching the target area, but were unable to identify anything. The German ships had in fact sailed shortly before the abortive attack took place and the flash of the bursting bombs led Admiral Lütjens to believe that his departure had not been noticed.

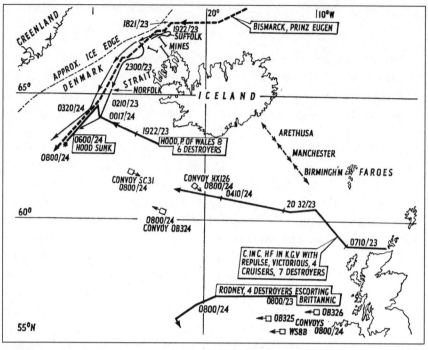

1. Operation Rheinübung on 23 May 1941. The sighting of the *Bismarck*.

2. Plan of action between HMS *Hood* and *Prince of Wales* and the German ships *Bismarck* and *Prinz Eugen* on 24 May.

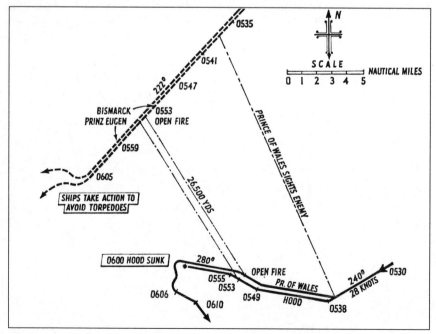

Chapter 2

British Home Fleet Sails

—⧖—

Admiral Tovey was anxiously awaiting further news of the enemy ships but, as has been mentioned, air reconnaissance proved useless in the prevailing weather. The Germans were similarly handicapped in obtaining information about the movements of British ships and a pilot who flew over Scapa Flow that day failed to notice the departure of the *Hood* and *Prince of Wales*, and belief that they were still in harbour reinforced Lütjen's opinion that he had made an unobserved departure. When, almost twenty-four hours had elapsed since the last sighting of the German ships, the Commanding Officer of the Royal Naval Air Station at Hatston in the Orkneys, Captain H. St. J. Fancourt RN ordered a twin-engined Maryland aircraft normally used for height-finding exercises to be prepared. It was manned by Lieutenant Commander (A) N.E. Goddard RNVR as Pilot, Commander G.A. Rotherham RN as Observer, and a radio operator and rear gunner chosen from a large number of volunteers. Although time was of the essence, it was most important to prepare the flight plan carefully to decide where on the Norwegian coast to make a landfall, and at what height to approach in order to avoid interception by the enemy's radar and by his fighters of which large numbers were believed to be stationed in that area. By 1600 all was ready and half an hour later the aircraft took off and succeeded in reaching the coast in fair visibility. An examination of Korsfiord showed that the anchorage was empty and after a look at Bergen where heavy A/A fire was encountered the news of the enemy's departure was signalled and reached Admiral Tovey at 1900. It was confirmed after the aircraft landed in the Shetlands at 1915. The Commander-in-Chief immediately gave orders for the ships remaining in Scapa to prepare for sea and to be ready to sail at 2200. He signalled Vice Admiral Holland not to call at Hvalfiord with his force, but to take up a position covering the patrols in the Denmark Straits and Iceland-Faroes passage, operating north of 62°N. He ordered the *Suffolk* to join the *Norfolk* on patrol, timing her departure so as to arrive in the Denmark Straits at the earliest time the *Bismarck* could arrive there in order to conserve fuel. The *Arethusa* was to support the *Manchester* and *Birmingham* in the Iceland-Faroes passage. Finally, he ordered the battle-cruiser *Repulse* to join him off the Butt of Lewis at 0700 the following morning.

At 2300 Admiral Tovey in his flagship the *King George V* accompanied by the cruisers *Galatea, Aurora, Kenya, Hermione*, and the destroyers *Inglefield* (Captain D), *Intrepid, Active, Punjabi, Nestor, Windsor* and *Lance* headed west from Scapa through the Pentland Firth. The *Lance* soon had to return on account of boiler trouble.

German Operation Orders

Admiral Lütjens' orders were clear. He was to attack enemy supply traffic in the Atlantic north of the Equator. The duration of the operation was left to his discretion. He was to proceed into the Atlantic via the Great Belt, the Skaggerak and the Norwegian Sea and was to attempt to break through unobserved. Even if the breakout were observed, the mission as defined above remained unaltered, but he was to avoid taking risks which might jeopardise the success of the operation and should avoid encounters with ships of superior or equal strength. If, however, such an encounter proved inevitable, then it should be an all-out (Ger. 'Unter vollen Einsatz') engagement. These instructions differed in one important respect from those he had received when in command of the battle-cruisers for their earlier sortie – they permitted attacks on escorted convoys unless these were escorted by a group of ships which together could be considered superior to the *Bismarck*. The Admiral was warned that the lightness of the nights would add to the difficulty of making an unobserved break-out, but that poor visibility to be expected along the ice edge in the Denmark Straits would be a factor in his favour, and although enemy patrols might be encountered in both the Iceland-Faroes passage and the Denmark Straits, the indications were that they were not yet equipped with radar.

Movements of the *Bismarck* and *Prinz Eugen*

The *Bismarck* and *Prinz Eugen* left Gdynia on the evening of 18 May escorted by minesweepers, aircraft and U-boats, made an uneventful passage through the Great Belt and Skagerrak and reached Kristiansand South on the evening of 20 May. Photographic reconnaissance of Scapa Flow showed that the Home Fleet was in harbour and air reconnaissance of the Denmark Straits, though hindered by bad weather, indicated that the ice edge lay between seventy and eighty miles from the North Cape (Iceland) thus giving a clear passage of twenty to thirty miles between it and the edge of the British minefield. At 0900 on 21 May the two ships entered Korsfiord near Bergen where they refuelled and where, as already mentioned, they were sighted by a British reconnaissance aircraft. The ships themselves did not observe this aircraft and it was only from a British message intercepted by the monitoring service that forenoon that the German Naval Staff learned that the movement of the ships had become known to the British. Leaving Korsfiord at 2300 with an escort of three destroyers, which were detached off Trondheim, they continued northward until reaching latitude 65°30'N when course was altered to the westward to pass north of Iceland with the intention of reaching the entrance to the Denmark Straits at about 0700 on 23 May. Although he had been informed that the presence of his ships in Korsfiord had become known to the enemy, Admiral Lütjens was optimistic about his chances of slipping through the British patrol line, as his meteorological officer had forecast fog which was just what he wanted. He had decided on using the Denmark Straits against the advice of Group North because he hoped it would afford him better chances of concealment, and so while Raeder was pleading with Hitler not to recall them, through the night of 22/23 May the two darkened ships headed west at 25 knots.

Interception
For Admiral Tovey the situation was full of uncertainty, which increased with every hour that passed without further news of the enemy ships. The weather was still preventing reconnaissance of the Norwegian coast but during daylight Sunderland flying boats and Hudson aircraft were keeping a constant watch over the passages between Iceland and the Faroes and also between the last-named and the Shetlands, despite strong head winds, rain squalls, heavy cloud and fog patches. Two Catalina flying boats despatched to cover the Denmark Straits were obliged to return owing to continuous heavy rain and thick cloud down to a height of 300 feet.

As soon as the *Repulse* screened by the destroyers *Legion, Saguenay* and *Assiniboine* joined his force at 0710 on 23 May the Commander-in-Chief altered the course of his force to north-west to take up a position covering the southern approach to the Faroes-Iceland passage. He had now disposed his fleet so as to cover both the possible channels by which the enemy might attempt to break out into the Atlantic, but as he had no information as to the time of his departure from Korsfiord, the possible area in which he might be, which was already large, was getting more so with every hour that passed. Weather again prevented air reconnaissance and in the prevailing poor visibility and with the limited forces available for patrolling, the chances of interception were anything but good. It was always possible that the enemy, acting on the assumption that his departure had been observed, might be waiting somewhere north of the Arctic Circle until he reckoned that some of the ships waiting to intercept him had to return to harbour to refuel. This possibility was very much to the fore in Admiral Tovey's mind.

When on 23 May the *Suffolk* joined his flag, Rear Admiral Wake-Walker instructed her to investigate the ice edge up to the minefield and then to patrol within radar range of the former in a north-easterly and south-westerly direction on a three hour beat, so as to be at the southern end at 2200 and every six hours thereafter. If the weather remained clear towards the land the *Norfolk* would keep fifteen miles to the east of her but if it thickened and she had to close the shore, the two ships were to rendezvous in a specified position at 1300 the following day to co-ordinate their movements. In fact the weather conditions in the Denmark Straits on the afternoon of the 23rd were unusual. It was clear over the ice pack and some ten miles of water adjoining it but the rest of the Straits as far as the Iceland coast was covered in thick mist. Because of this, the *Suffolk*, on reaching the top of the minefield, steamed further to the east than would otherwise have been prudent, and kept close to the edge of the mist to have cover handy in case of need.

At noon on that day, the *Bismarck* and *Prinz Eugen* began the most risky part of their voyage as they shaped course to pass between the ice edge and the minefield off the north-west coast of Iceland. The weather described above was not at all what Admiral Lütjens had been led to expect. At 1900 the two ships reached the narrowest part of the channel and may well have begun to feel that luck was on their side, but twenty-two minutes later, a lookout covering the stern sector in the *Suffolk*, which had just turned to the south-west after investigating the ice edge, reported two ships bearing 020°7 miles. A quick look through binoculars confirmed the presence of the *Bismarck* and another similar looking vessel steering to the southwest. Captain R.M. Ellis RN commanding the *Suffolk* immediately increased to full speed and turned his ship towards a gap in the minefield and took cover in the mist until the enemy ships had passed, at the same time sending out an enemy report.

Force H Ordered to Sail
The news that the two enemy ships had been sighted heading for the Atlantic increased the Admiralty's concern for the safety of the eleven British convoys at sea there, which included the troop convoy of five ships designated WS.8B, which had left the Clyde on 21 May and which the *Victorious* and *Repulse* were to have escorted during its passage to the Middle East. It now had only an escort of two cruisers and eight destroyers. At 0500/24 a signal was therefore sent to Vice Admiral Sir James Somerville, flag officer commanding Force H based on Gibraltar, to sail and steer to the northward to cover this convoy. Force H comprised the modernised battle-cruiser HMS *Renown* (flagship), the carrier HMS *Ark Royal*, the 6in gun cruiser HMS *Sheffield* and the destroyers *Faulknor*, *Foresight*, *Forester*, *Foxhound*, *Fury* and *Hesperus*. Although the *Renown* was no match for the *Bismarck*, this force was destined to play a significant part in her demise.

Shadowing Tactics
When Coastal Command received news of the sighting of the German ships, a Sunderland flying boat and a Hudson reconnaissance aircraft were sent from Iceland to assist in maintaining touch with the enemy. The Hudson failed to find them and returned, but the flying boat held on throughout the night though it did not make contact with the *Suffolk* until the following morning. The cruiser had recently been fitted with Type 284 Radar (see Appendix II) which although trainable, had a blind spot over the stern, otherwise she would probably have located the *Bismarck* earlier than she did. As soon as the enemy ships had drawn ahead and were on a forward bearing, Captain Ellis took up a position for shadowing. An hour later he was joined by the *Norfolk* which at the time of the sighting was some 15 miles away to the south-west. The cruiser sighting flagship was equipped with radar Type 286P which had

two fixed aerials and so could only take ranges on an ahead bearing. In closing in she was less fortunate than her consort. The *Bismarck* had by now picked up the pulses of the *Suffolk*'s radar transmissions and was on the alert. At 2030 when the *Norfolk* appeared out of the mist at a range of about six miles, she was greeted with five salvoes from the battleship's main armament and obliged to beat a hasty retreat. Fortunately she was not hit and sent out an enemy report timed 2032/23. The enemy ships were hugging the ice edge and thus forcing the *Suffolk* to keep more or less astern of them, so the *Norfolk* took up position on their port quarter, relying on a plot of the *Suffolk*'s regular reports to warn her of any sudden change in the enemy's course and/or speed. Although the German ships were fitted with search radar known as DT equipment, they did not have an accurate gunnery set and so were unable to drive off the shadowers using radar-controlled blind fire. On discovering that his ships had been sighted, Admiral Lütjens increased their speed to 28 knots in the hope presumably of outdistancing his pursuers and he ordered the *Prinz Eugen* to take station ahead of the *Bismarck* and so clear the range for the latter's after guns should the shadowers approach too close. The German report of the operation refers to the surprise occasioned by the discovery that the British ships were equipped with 'excellently functioning radar equipment' which it is claimed was 'of decisive importance for the further course of the operation' and which deprived them of the advantage to be gained from poor visibility.

Although the Admiralty picked up the *Suffolk*'s enemy report, Admiral Tovey remained in ignorance of the event until he received the *Norfolk*'s report timed 2032. Vice Admiral Holland, however, had received one of the *Suffolk*'s reports timed 1939 and it showed the enemy ships to be about 300 miles to the northward of him, bearing 005°. He was thus very favourably placed to cut them off if they continued on a south-westerly course. At 2054, therefore, he ordered his force to increase speed to 27 knots and to steer a course of 295° which he estimated would enable him to make contact with them during the early hours of 24 May. The steady flow of reports coming in from the shadowing cruisers enabled an accurate plot to be kept of the enemy's movements and minor adjustments to be made to bring about an encounter at a time and on a bearing favourable to the British ships. So far as the *Hood* was concerned it was imperative to close as quickly as possible to a range at which the trajectory of the enemy's 15in shell would be more nearly horizontal, that is, about 12,000 yards, because of the known weakness of that ship's horizontal armour. The *Prince of Wales*, on the other hand, not only had a 15in armoured belt but a 6in armoured deck and was considered safe from vital hits down to a range of about 13,000 yards. It was difficult to reconcile the conflicting claims of an old battle-cruiser and a new battleship but, on balance, the Admiral decided on an approach from fine on the *Bismarck*'s bow which would give a high closing rate and enable the action to be fought at a comparatively short range. Just before midnight the cruiser's shadowing reports suddenly ceased. A snowstorm had enveloped the German ships and their shadowers. It caused considerable clutter on the radar screens and in the semi-twilight of an Arctic night in May produced some strange mirage effects. The cruiser captains were aware that the enemy might, at any time, decide to reverse his course and that, if they failed to react promptly to such a move, they would be blown out of the water by his big guns. When, therefore, the lookouts in the *Suffolk* saw what looked like the dark shadow of a ship bearing down on them Captain Ellis immediately put his helm hard over and turned to a reciprocal course. When he realised that he had been deceived and turned back to resume the chase, he had dropped so far astern that radar contact had been lost. It took him three hours to regain it. The *Norfolk* too lost touch and the sudden cessation of information appears to have led Vice Admiral Holland to assume that the enemy ships had taken drastic action to throw off their shadowers either by a reversal of course to re-enter the Denmark Straits or by a major alteration to the south or south-east. At 2359, therefore, he ordered his force to steer north and to reduce speed to 25 knots. What his exact motives were in making this turn will never be known. There is some support for the belief that he may have been contemplating a night action because, at 0015, he signalled that contact with the enemy might be expected any time after 0140/24 and ordered his ships to prepare for action. He must, however, have been aware that if the enemy ships were continuing along their last reported course and at the same speed, he was placing himself in a position of tactical disadvantage by allowing them to gain so much bearing knowing that his ships did not have a sufficient margin of speed to regain it. It is also possible, of course, that the plot in the *Hood* showed the *Bismarck* to be further off and more to the eastward than she was, since at that time there was no opportunity of co-ordinating positions with *Norfolk* and *Suffolk*.

At 0031 Admiral Holland informed his force that, if the enemy ships had not been sighted by 0210, he would probably alter course to the southward (180°) until the cruisers regained touch and that he intended both ships to engage the *Bismarck*, leaving the *Prinz Eugen* to the two cruisers. Admiral Wake-Walker, however, was not informed of the part he was expected to play in the forthcoming action; in fact, his first intimation of the presence of Admiral Holland's force in his vicinity was when at 0445 he intercepted a message from the destroyer *Icarus* giving her position and that of the *Achates*, which showed them to be some distance astern of the *Norfolk*. At 0147 Admiral Holland told his destroyers to continue to search to the northward should the battle-cruisers (*sic*) alter course to 200° at 0205. There were now only four of them, the *Anthony* and *Antelope* having been detached at 1400/23 to fuel in Iceland.

At 0203, as the brief Arctic night was beginning to lift, no further news of the enemy having been received, the force altered course to 200°, approximately parallel to the enemy's last reported course. At the same time the Admiral told the *Prince of Wales* to use her gunnery radar Type 284 to search for the enemy who, unknown to him was 35 miles away to the north-west. When Captain Leach asked permission to use his search radar Type 281 instead as the gunnery set would not bear right aft, permission was refused for reasons it is difficult to conjecture. It may have been because all-round search of Type 281 was more liable to interception and direction finding than the more directional beam of Type 284. Also this latter set worked on 50cm wave length and a much higher frequency than any set used by the Germans at that time.

As suddenly as she had lost it, the *Suffolk* regained contact with the *Bismarck* at 0247 and again began to transmit a series of shadowing reports. These, together with Direction Finding bearings of the cruisers taken by the *Prince of Wales*, must have enabled the *Hood* to make an accurate assessment of the enemy's ship's position, course and speed, which would have shown that they were still steering south-south-west at 28 knots. This must have made it plain to Admiral Holland, if he was not already aware of it, that he had lost so much bearing on the enemy that an end on approach was now impossible. Matters were made even worse when, at 0320, Admiral Lütjens, in conformity with his policy of hugging the ice edge, altered course to the westward (230°) thereby putting the British force only fifteen degrees before his beam, distant 25 miles, although at this stage he was still unaware of its presence. Had Admiral Holland been forty or fifty miles ahead of his opponent, this unexpected move on the enemy's part could perhaps have been allowed for but now it was too late, especially as it apparently took some time for it to be noticed. It was not until 0340 that he altered the course of his force to 240° to conform and at 0353 increased speed to 28 knots. The two forces now raced along on slightly converging courses. At 0430 visibility had increased to about 12 miles and ten minutes later the *Prince of Wales* was ordered to prepare her Walrus amphibious aircraft for flying. Water in the fuel caused delay so that it was not ready in time and after being damaged by splinters during the action it was jettisoned. At 0510 instant readiness for action was assumed in both ships and at 0537 the *Prince of Wales* reported 'Enemy in sight distant 17 miles' just as Admiral Holland executed the signal directing both ships to turn 40 degrees to starboard together (280°) to close the range. Four minutes later he stationed the *Prince of Wales* on a bearing of 080°, that is, approximately at right angles to the bearing of the enemy. At 0530 the *Bismarck* and *Prinz Eugen* had sighted the smoke of two ships below the horizon to the south–south-east and both prepared for action.

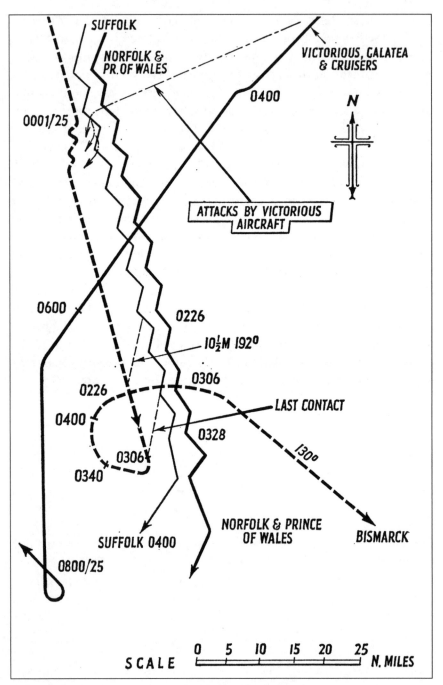

SUFFOLK

NORFOLK &
PR. OF WALES

VICTORIOUS, GALATEA
& CRUISERS

0400

0001/25

N

ATTACKS BY VICTORIOUS
AIRCRAFT

0600

0226

$10\frac{1}{2}$M 192°

0226

0306

0400

LAST CONTACT

0306

0328

130°

0340

NORFOLK & PRINCE
OF WALES

BISMARCK

SUFFOLK 0400

0800/25

SCALE

0   5   10   15   20   25

N. MILES

3. *Bismarck* lost after torpedo attacks by *Victorious*' aircraft.

Chapter 3

Action and Reaction

—ᵐ—

At 0549/24 Admiral Holland ordered his two ships to turn together 20° to starboard which brought them on to a course of 300°, and to concentrate their fire on the left-hand enemy ship, erroneously believing that it was the *Bismarck*, the similarity of the silhouettes of the two ships deceiving him. Fortunately, the Gunnery Control officer in the *Prince of Wales*, on his own initiative, realised that a mistake had been made and trained his guns on to the *Bismarck* only seconds before opening fire. Admiral Holland quickly realised his error and signalled 'Shift target right' but it does not appear that this order reached the Gunnery Control officer in the *Hood*. At 0552½ the *Hood* opened fire at an estimated range of 25,000 yards, to be followed half a minute by the *Prince of Wales*. The turn of 20° towards the enemy made by the British ships just prior to opening fire closed their 'A' arcs, that is to say that the after turrets in both ships could not be trained sufficiently far forward to bear on the target. This meant that only four of the *Hood*'s eight 15in and six of the *Prince of Wales*'s ten 14in guns were in action at a crucial time. To make matters worse, one of the last named was only capable of firing one round because of a defect in the loading mechanism. The enemy, from whom the British ships were bearing just before his beam, being under no such handicap, was able to bring the full weight of his armament to bear against them when, at 0555, the two ships opened fire which was concentrated on the *Hood*. The range was closing rapidly and, at the same instant as the enemy opened fire, Admiral Holland ordered his two ships to turn together 20° to port and so enable 'A' arcs to be reopened. When the signal was executed the *Prince of Wales* had just fired her ninth salvo, having straddled the *Bismarck* with her sixth. The first salvo from the last-named ship fell ahead of the *Hood* and the second astern, but the third was a straddle.

Meanwhile, the *Prinz Eugen*, with the more rapid rate of fire of her 8in guns, soon found the range and one of her shells is believed to have been responsible for starting a fire in the *Hood* amongst the ready-use UP ammunition, ten tons of which was housed in thin steel lockers. The greater part of this was on the boat deck, having been embarked during the ship's brief refit at Devonport in April 1940. As an A/A device the UP (unrotated projectile) rocket was not a success and was later withdrawn from the fleet; however, the presence of such a large amount of insufficiently protected explosive in such an exposed position endangered the ship. The fire spread rapidly forward but whether or not it contributed to the impending disaster will never be known, but it seems unlikely.

At 0600 Admiral Holland had a signal flying directing his ships to turn a further 20° to port together, the *Hood* had just fired a full salvo and the *Bismarck* her fifth, when horrified watchers in the *Prince of Wales* saw a pillar of flame leap in the air from the after part of the *Hood*, followed by a tremendous explosion which rent the ship in two, while a mass of debris soared skywards; then her bow and stern reared up and slid slowly back into the sea, shrouded in a pall of smoke. In a matter of minutes, all that remained of the famous battle-cruiser known throughout the Royal Navy as 'the mighty *Hood*' was a mass of wreckage. Out of a ship's company of 1,418 there were only three survivors, whose rescue an hour and a half later is described below. Another mute witness to the disaster was the Sunderland flying boat from Iceland, which had finally succeeded in making contact with the *Suffolk* just before the action began. After seeing the *Hood* blow up, the pilot closed in on the *Bismarck* in order to identify her and came under heavy A/A fire, but he was able to observe that she was now leaving a broad track of oil, proof of damage received. He emerged from cloud cover just in time to see the *Hood*'s bows disappear and, flying over the spot a moment or two later, he saw an empty raft painted red surrounded by wreckage in the middle of a large patch of oil. What exactly set off the explosion which caused the *Hood* to disintegrate can only be surmised, but it would seem that a shell must have penetrated one of her magazines. In a letter to *The Times* dated 26 May 1941, the late Admiral of the Fleet Lord Chatfield who, as First Sea Lord and Chief of the Naval Staff from 1933 to 1938, had fought tenaciously but unsuccessfully to persuade the government of the day to approve a modernisation programme for the obsolescent capital ships in the British fleet and who was, therefore, in a strong position to comment on the disaster, made these five points:

• The *Hood* was not the most powerful warship afloat. True, she was the largest but she was constructed 22 years before the *Bismarck*. In those 22 years engineering science and the power-weight ratio changed beyond imagination.

• It cannot be truly said that 'she was destroyed by a lucky hit.' There are numerous magazines in a capital ship in addition to the four large ones which lie beneath the main turrets. If, therefore, a heavy shell penetrates the armour at the angle of descent given by long ranges, the chance of one of the magazines being ignited is quite considerable.

• The *Hood* was the most powerful ship of her speed that could be constructed in those days. But, after the war, the sailor made up his mind, after much experiment, that a very fast ship cannot afford to sacrifice armour to gain that speed.

• So, in the Nelson class, speed was sacrificed to ensure protection against sudden annihilation by shell, torpedo or bomb.

• Since the Nelson was built, modern engineering has closed the gap between the two factors.

And he concluded:

'The *Hood* was destroyed because she had to fight a ship 22 years more modern than herself.'

Captain Leach in the *Prince of Wales* had to swing his ship rapidly to starboard to avoid the wreck of the *Hood*. Up until then he had been firing at the *Bismarck* virtually undisturbed but the latter quickly and accurately shifted the fire of both her main and secondary armament to the new target which she believed was the *King George V* and which was soon surrounded by towering shell splashes, making it difficult for the British battleship's control officer to spot his own fall of shot. It was only a matter of a minute before a 15in shell struck the bridge structure, wrecking it and killing or wounding everyone on it except Captain Leach and his Chief Yeoman of Signals, both of whom, however, were momentarily dazed. The shell did not burst until it emerged on the far side of the bridge structure, which was fortunate. During the next few minutes the *Prince of Wales* received a further six hits, three from 15in and three from 8in shell. One of the first named struck the starboard foremost 5.25in director, putting it out of action, another hit the aircraft crane and shattered both wings of the aircraft, the body of which was immediately ditched, while the third pierced the ship's side below the waterline and, after passing through several bulkheads, came to rest without exploding alongside a diesel dynamo room. Two 8in shells hit on the waterline aft, causing a great deal of flooding, while a third entered a 5.25in shell handing room but fortunately again failed to explode. The persistent teething troubles from which the battleship's main armament had suffered throughout the action now began seriously to affect her fire power and, instead of being able to fire five gun salvoes, they were mostly only of three. The contractors' men, who were still onboard, did their utmost in the totally unforeseen circumstances with which they were confronted to keep the guns in action but they only achieved partial success. The range was now down to 14,500 yards and with the enemy's rate and accuracy of fire still apparently unimpaired, at 0613 Captain Leach decided to break off the action and retire under cover of smoke. He altered course to 160° and during the turn the shell ring of the after 14in turret which was still firing at the *Bismarck* jammed and it was not until 0720 that two of the guns were back in action and another hour before the other two could be loaded. Captain Leach gave three main reasons for breaking off the engagement:

- the mechanical troubles which prevented the main armament from producing a full output;
- his ship had only just reached the stage of being reasonably fit to take part in services operations;
- the likelihood of a decisive concentration being effected later.

He went on to say that he did not consider it sound tactics to continue single-handed the engagement with the two German ships, both of which might be expected to be at the peak of their efficiency. As a result of the damage she had received the *Prince of Wales* had shipped 400 tons of water and her speed was reduced to 27 knots. Rear Admiral Wake-Walker, who had now succeeded to the command of the force, fully approved Captain Leach's action. At 0630 he signalled his intention of maintaining touch and he ordered the *Prince of Wales* to open out to a distance of ten miles on a bearing of 110° so that he could fall back on her, if attacked. At 0637 he ordered the destroyers *Electra, Echo, Icarus* and *Achates* to search for survivors of the *Hood*. They were 30 miles north of the scene of the action as a result of Admiral Holland's decision to detach them when he turned south and it was 0745 before they reached the position where the *Hood* had blown up. A dramatic account of the rescue of the only three survivors is given in the book, HMS *Electra*, a ship with a war record unique in the annals of naval warfare. After describing how she raced south expecting to find hundreds of survivors in boats, on rafts or swimming about in the water, those on her bridge sighted 'quite suddenly, on the rolling swell, a large patch of oil ahead, a tangled pile of small wreckage ... *and that was all* ... far over to starboard we saw three men – two of them swimming, one on a raft. But in the chilling waters around them there was no other sign of life.'[8] After recovering the three men, one of whom was a Midshipman, the *Electra* and the other destroyers searched the area until 0900 when they set course for Hvalfiord where they arrived at 2000 that night.

The *Bismarck* did not attempt to continue the action. She had received two severe hits and one minor one from the *Prince of Wales*'s guns, one of which pierced compartment 13/14 and put No. 4 dynamo out of action, as well as causing a slight leak in number 2 boiler room, the other entering compartment 20/21, pierced a fuel tank causing a serious leak of oil as well as contaminating fuel in adjacent tanks. Five men were wounded and the ship's speed reduced to 28 knots. The *Prinz Eugen*, believed to have been the target of the *Hood*'s guns during her brief period in action, escaped undamaged. Admiral Lütjens was now faced with a difficult decision. He could either continue the action with the risk of further damage or attempt to break back through the Denmark Straits in the hope of reaching a German port. Alternatively, he could continue into the Atlantic in the hope of throwing off his shadowers and then make for a port on the west coast of France, bearing in mind that only at St. Nazaire was there a dry dock large enough to take the *Bismarck*. He evidently decided on the second course and at 0901 made a signal to this effect to Group West at the same time reporting the damage suffered by his flagship. Admiral Raeder says that he fully agreed with the decision and he stoutly defended Lütjens's action when, on 6 June, he reported to Hitler the tragic outcome of the operation. Hitler, on the other hand, criticised him for not continuing the action and finishing off the *Prince of Wales*. A German historian has written:

'If he had had the slightest suspicion that his target was the *Prince of Wales* which was still in the testing stage, manned by a totally inexperienced crew with some shipyard personnel still onboard, and working to overcome 'bugs', he would hardly have permitted her to escape.'[9]

Be that as it may and even if, as another writer suggests,[10] Captain Lindemann did not agree with his Admiral's decision though he too thought he had been engaged with the *King George V*, it must remain a matter for speculation, since no one with a knowledge of what was in the Admiral's mind survived.

When the news of the loss of the *Hood* reached the Admiralty, a number of dispositions were made to meet possible eventualities. At 0120/24 the cruisers *Manchester, Birmingham* and *Arethusa* were ordered to proceed with despatch to patrol off Langanaes (north-east point of Iceland); the battleship *Rodney* which, with four destroyers, was escorting the west-bound liner *Britannic*, was ordered at 1022/24 to close the enemy on a westerly course, leaving one destroyer with the *Britannic*. Detailing the *Eskimo* for this duty, she took the *Somali, Tartar* and *Mashona* with her. She was on her way to Boston, USA for a much needed refit and had onboard a number of officer and rating passengers who included some cases of shell-shock and invalids bound for hospitals in Canada. Her upper deck was encumbered with several cases of spare parts needed during the refit and two extra large ones, each containing an eight-barrelled Pom-Pom mounting. She had not been refitted for over two years and her main engines and boilers were full of leaks as a result of prolonged high speed steaming during the first months of the war. But, despite all these handicaps, she was to play a very important part in the events about to take place.

The battleship *Ramillies* escorting an eastbound convoy, at 1144/24 was ordered to place herself westward of the enemy ship, who was estimated to be 900 miles to the north of her, and the battleship *Revenge* at Halifax was instructed at 1917/24 to sail and close the position of the enemy. The cruiser *Edinburgh* on patrol in mid-Atlantic was ordered at 1250/24 to close the enemy and take over as a relief shadower.

Throughout the forenoon of the 24th, the *Bismarck* proceeded in a south-westerly direction trying hard by frequent alterations of course to throw off the persistent British cruisers. The visibility was variable, between two and seventeen miles, but the *Suffolk*, with the help of her radar, maintained station on her starboard quarter and so, forestalling any attempt on the part of the enemy to break back along the ice edge unobserved, while the *Norfolk* and the *Prince of Wales* kept on the port quarter. At 1320 the *Bismarck* altered course to south and reduced speed to 24 knots. This was welcome news to Admiral Tovey who, up until then, had been anxious lest the enemy ships should turn westwards and rendezvous with a tanker off Greenland where, unknown to him, there were in fact two waiting, 120 and 200 miles south of Cape Farewell. The Commander-in-Chief was not aware of the extent of the damage received by the *Bismarck* during the action other than that she was leaving an appreciable trail of oil. There was, of course, the possibility that Admiral Lütjens was leading the British ships towards a concentration of U-boats but it seemed unlikely that he was aware of the presence of other heavy ships at sea in the area. The chances of interception by the *King George V* had now much improved but it was important to reduce the *Bismarck*'s speed to make sure of bringing her to action. At 1440 Admiral Tovey detached Rear Admiral A.T.B. Curteis commanding the 2nd Cruiser Squadron, with his flag in the 6in gun cruiser *Galatea* with the carrier *Victorious* and the cruisers *Aurora*, *Kenya* and *Hermione*, with orders to sail to within 100 miles of the *Bismarck* as soon as possible and launch a Torpedo/Bomber attack on her. It appeared to him that, if the *Bismarck* continued on her present course and at the same speed, he would be able to make contact with her at about 0900/25, half an hour after sunrise when the light would be favourable to an approach from the eastward.

At 1535 a Catalina aircraft which was in sight from the *Norfolk* sighted, without apparently being seen herself, and reported the enemy battleship as 15 miles ahead preceded by the *Prinz Eugen*. About this time Admiral Lütjens made his first attempt to detach the *Prinz Eugen* but did not managed to so that the two ships found themselves in company again. At 1711 Admiral Wake-Walker ordered the *Prince of Wales* to take station ahead of the *Norfolk* with a view to trying to slow down the enemy by attacking her from astern and at 1809 he ordered the *Suffolk* to close in to give miles. His plan was, however, frustrated by the enemy. At about 1830 a rainsquall enveloped the enemy ships and Admiral Lütjens decided this was the moment to make a second attempt to detach the *Prinz Eugen*. At 1839 he ordered the *Bismarck* to reverse her course and round on her shadowers. At the time the *Suffolk* was about 13 miles to the north of her and fortunately was on the lookout for such a move. She put her helm hard over and swung round on an opposite course on which she steadied just as the *Bismarck*, emerging from the mist, opened fire on her. The shots fell short, although two near misses started rivets in the side plating aft. She made smoke and opened fire, being supported at long range by the *Norfolk* and *Prince of Wales*, two of whose guns again went out of action. Her object achieved, the *Bismarck* broke off the action and turned west, later resuming a southerly course.

The German Naval High Command had suspended all U-boat operations against shipping for the duration of Operation Rheinübung in case the submarines were needed to co-operate with the surface ships and an experienced U-boat officer had been appointed to Admiral Lütjens's staff. Presumably on his advance, at 1442 the Admiral had ordered U-boats to concentrate 340 miles south of Cape Farewell (Greenland) at dawn on the 25th, hoping to lead his persistent shadowers over them. Group West had also suggested that he should make for some remote area and lie low for a while, but the Admiral seems to have discarded both these projects when he realised how serious was the loss of fuel as a result of the damage sustained during the action. In any case, it seemed impossible from his pursuers and at 2056 he signalled that he was proceeding direct to Brest owing to the fuel situation.

Meanwhile, at 1509, Rear Admiral Curteis had taken the ships assigned to him under his orders and, parting company with the Commander-in-Chief, was proceeding at 28 knots to carry out his instructions, hoping to be in a position to launch an attack on the enemy battleship at 2100. Although, however, the navigating officer of the *Galatea* had obtained an astronomical fix at 2000, it had not been possible to co-ordinate the geographical position of his force with that of the shadowing cruisers, further the westerly side-step made by the *Bismarck* after her brush with the *Prince of Wales* and the two cruisers soon made it evident that the force would not reach a position within 100 miles of the enemy before about 2300. Nevertheless, Admiral Curteis decided to launch the striking force at 2200 when he estimated he would be about 120 miles away from the target. At 2208 the *Victorious* altered course to 300° and reduced speed to 15 knots to fly off her nine Swordfish aircraft of 825 squadron, each armed with an 18in torpedo fitted with a Duplex pistol and set to run at a depth of 31 feet. The weather was squally with occasional showers, the wind being fresh from the north-west and visibility good. But, as seen from the flying deck, the prospect was not encouraging, the sea looked dark and forbidding under a leaden sky and scudding clouds. The squadron led by Lieutenant Commander Eugen Esmonde RN (later to earn a posthumous VC for his gallant attack against the *Scharnhorst*) set course 225° at 85 knots and sighted the *Bismarck* through a gap in the clouds at 2330, having picked her up by radar three minutes previously, then the cloud thickened and she was lost to view. A United States coastguard cutter in the vicinity caused some confusion but, with the help of the *Norfolk*, the battleship was relocated and at 2350 the formation broke cloud to deliver its attack. The *Bismarck* sighted the aircraft at a range of six miles and opened a heavy barrage fire but the attacks were pressed home with great gallantry from all directions by eight of the nine aircraft and it was believed that a hit was scored on the battleship's starboard side abreast the bridge. The German report admitting this stated that it had no effect on the ship's combat readiness, which was true, but it appears that the violent turns made by the ship to avoid the torpedoes, coupled with the heavy gunfire, opened up the leak in number 2 boiler room which had to be abandoned and speed was temporarily reduced to 16 knots. A Fulmar reconnaissance aircraft flown off at 2300 observed a column of black smoke rising from the ship which was no doubt due to the sudden reduction in speed and reported that she seemed to have slowed down. Great difficulty was experienced in recovering the strike aircraft due to a breakdown of *Victorious*'s homing beacon and searchlights had to be burned, but by 0215/15, all aircraft except two Fulmars had been recovered and the crews of these last two were subsequently picked up.

Contact Lost with the *Bismarck*

To Admiral Tovey the news of a probable hit on the *Bismarck* was most welcome, but it would not be known for some time whether or not it had reduced her speed. While awaiting confirmation of this, a most untoward event occurred. The *Suffolk*, which had a better radar set, had been ordered at 0145 to act independently while the *Norfolk*, with the *Prince of Wales* astern, followed to give close support. The *Bismarck* was now steering a course of 160° at a speed of 16 knots. At 0229 she bore 192° distant 10½ miles from the *Suffolk* which was zig-zagging 30 degrees on either side of the mean line of advance and losing touch on the outward legs but regaining it on the inward ones. The effect on a tired crew was to engender a feeling of over confidence. After contact at 0306 the

Suffolk turned away, at which instant the *Bismarck* altered course sharply to starboard so that when the cruiser, after the customary ten minutes on the outward leg turned inwards there was no sign of the enemy. By 0401, when Captain Ellis was obliged to recognise the disagreeable fact, that the battleship had given him the slip, he reported the fact adding that he was acting on the assumption that she had turned west. The *Norfolk* herself had not had contact with the *Bismarck* for two hours and at 0552 Admiral Wake-Walker asked Admiral Tovey if the *Victorious* could carry out an air search in this direction at dawn. The *Bismarck* had, in fact, turned almost a complete circle from south through west to north and east, finally steadying on a course of approximately 130°.

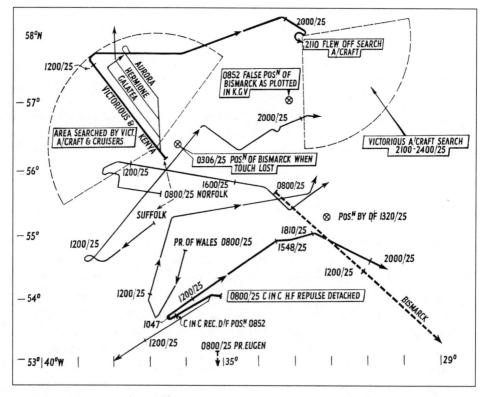

4. Movements of British Forces after losing touch with *Bismarck* 0800–2000 on 25 May.

Chapter 4

Pursuit

—ᗰ—

All hopes of bringing the *Bismarck* to action on the forenoon of 25 May faded with the receipt of the news that contact had been lost, which reached Admiral Tovey at 0605 that morning. It appeared to him that she might be doing one of three things:

• making a rendezvous with a tanker, possibly off the east coast of Greenland, or somewhere further south, like the Azores or Canary Islands;
• making for a dockyard on the west coast of France or possibly an Italian port in the Mediterranean;
• returning to Germany for repairs.

In default of further information, it had to be assumed that her speed was unimpaired and, as she had complete freedom of movement, a wide area of search would have to be covered if all possible courses of action were to be met. For this, the forces at his disposal were quite inadequate, especially long-range aircraft which were in very short supply at that time. He therefore had to decide which of the above courses was the most dangerous from the British point of view and it was clearly the first option, since with her fuel tanks replenished the *Bismarck* would be able to start operations against shipping which it must be supposed was the object of her sortie. He therefore decided to concentrate his efforts on searching an area between south through west to north-west from the *Bismarck*'s last reported position. As already noted, Rear Admiral Wake-Walker's two cruisers had anticipated this action, the *Suffolk* having started to search in a south-westerly direction (230°) at 25 knots, while the *Norfolk* searched to the westward at daylight. At 0630 the *Prince of Wales* was detached to join the Commander-in-Chief.

At 0630 Admiral Tovey ordered Rear Admiral Curteis, who was now steering with his force towards the *Bismarck*'s last reported position, to direct the *Victorious* to carry out a dawn search to the north-west and to spread his cruisers and sweep in that direction. The message was received at 0716 just as the carrier was preparing to carry out an air search to the eastward, timed to begin at 0730. During the night five Fulmars had been launched to maintain touch with the enemy, but without success. Two of these, as already mentioned, had failed to return, so only seven Swordfish were now available to carry out the search and these were launched at 0810 with orders to cover a sector between 280° and 040° to a depth of 100 miles to comply with the Commander-in-Chief's instructions. The battle-cruiser *Repulse* reported that she was running short of fuel, so at 0906 Admiral Tovey detached her with orders to proceed to Newfoundland to replenish, covering on passage part of the westerly search sector. Then at 1047 information was received which called for a complete change of plan but, before considering it, it is necessary to review the movements of the other ships at sea in the Atlantic.

The battleship *Rodney,* Captain F.H.G. Dalrymple-Hamilton RN, which had been steering to the south-west to intercept the *Bismarck*, and which was at this time 350 miles south-east of her last reported position, received the signal reporting that contact had been lost. Finding that she was in an excellent position to cut off the enemy ship were she heading for a French port or even one in northern Spain, her Captain decided to cruise in his present area until further news was received.

The battleship *Ramillies*, Captain A.D. Read RN, the top speed of which was not more than 19 knots, was some 400 miles south of the position where the *Bismarck* had given her shadowers the slip and was steering to the north-west in accordance with the instructions previously received from the Admiralty. The cruiser *Edinburgh*, Captain C.M. Blackman RN, 300 miles south-east of the *Ramillies*, was steering towards the enemy's last reported position and in so doing was covering part of the south-east sector of the enemy's possible line of advance. Further south the cruiser *London*, Captain R.M. Servaes RN, was searching for a possible enemy supply ship in the Canary Islands area.

Vice Admiral Somerville with Force H was pressing on to the northward and at 1300/25 was 320 miles due west of Cape Finisterre and so in a good position to intercept the *Bismarck*, should she be heading for Brest or Ferrol, which he thought was a likely alternative.

Onboard the *Bismarck* at 0800/25 Admiral Lütjens, still unaware that the shadowing cruisers had lost touch apparently because radar pulses were still being picked up, though this did not necessarily mean that the sender was receiving any echo, despatched an amplifying account of the action with the *Hood* which took some thirty minutes to transmit. Watchful British Direction Finding stations took bearings of this transmission which, when plotted, showed that the *Bismarck* was well east of her last reported position. Unfortunately, instead of giving Admiral Tovey the position thus obtained, the actual bearings were passed to him and these were plotted on a Mercators chart, although bearings obtained by radio follow a great circle path along the surface of the earth. The false position thus obtained, put the *Bismarck* 200 miles north of her true position and from this the Commander-in-Chief deduced that she was trying to return to Germany through the Iceland-Faroes channel. So, at 1047, shortly after detaching the *Repulse*, he altered the course of his force to the north-east and set off in pursuit, at the same time telling all Home Fleet ships to adjust their searches accordingly.

On receipt of the Commander-in-Chief's signal, Rear Admiral Curteis with his four cruisers turned to the eastward (085°), leaving the *Victorious*, the search of whose aircraft to the north-west had proved fruitless, to recover them. At 1107 she landed on six Swordfish, one having failed to return and, after calling he missing aircraft for some time, she also turned east and prepared to launch a further search. Other ships reacted similarly. The *Prince of Wales*, steering to close the fleet flagship, altered course for the Denmark Straits; the *Ramillies* changed course from north to east-north-east, although she could not hope to overtake the much faster enemy ship; the *Rodney*, which at 1108 had been ordered by the Admiralty to act on the assumption that the *Bismarck* was making for Brest, was in a quandary but at 1200, having regained her three destroyers which had dropped back owing to bad weather, set off on a course of 055°. Two and a half hours later, at 1428, the Admiralty ordered the *Rodney* to comply with the Commander-in-Chief's message timed 1047, which she was now doing, then at 1805 the message timed 1428 was cancelled and she was told to act on the assumption that the enemy ship was making for a French port. This series of signals shows the difficulty experienced in reaching a conclusion regarding the *Bismarck*'s most probable course of action. Rear Admiral Wake-Walker was convinced in his own mind that the

Bismarck would be making for Brest so he compromised by steering a course a little to the south of east (100°), while the *Suffolk* steered towards Iceland. The cruiser *Edinburgh* apparently too far south to be of much use in what now appeared to be a stern chase, began a curve of search in case the enemy should be making for Brest.

Admiral Somerville, whose Force H was not strictly a part of the Home Fleet and who had intercepted Admiral Tovey's message timed 1047, now received one from the Admiralty timed 1100 ordering him to assume that the *Bismarck* was making for Brest, altered course to 337° and instructed the *Ark Royal* to prepare to carry out an extensive air search. Meanwhile, that afternoon three Catalina aircraft of Coastal Command began a search of the area through which it was considered probable the *Bismarck* might be steaming. They continued their searches for an average of just over 20 hours but failed to sight the enemy although one of them sighted a warship during the night which could not be identified and low cloud prevented the use of a parachute flare.

At 1320 the Admiralty obtained bearings of an enemy transmission which was, in fact, made by a U-boat reporting having sighted the *Victorious* and which appeared to fit in with the assumption that the *Bismarck* was making for the French coast. It might have been suspected from the radio frequency employed that it was unlikely that it emanated from the *Bismarck*, but it was passed to Admiral Tovey, for what it was worth, and reached him at 1530. But an hour earlier he had intercepted the Admiralty's signal timed 1428 to the *Rodney* telling her to comply with his instructions to search to the north-eastward, so he was in some doubt as to what the Admiralty's appreciation of the enemy's intended movement really was. Meanwhile, the error in the plotting of the 0852 D/F position had been discovered and this, taken in conjunction with the one just received, seemed to indicate that the *Bismarck* was not seeking to return to Germany by the Iceland-Faroes passage. After a thorough re-appreciation in the light of the little information available, he decided at 1810 to alter course to the east-south-eastward (118°). Just over an hour later, at 1924, the Admiralty informed all ships that it was now the considered opinion of the naval staff that the *Bismarck* was making for a French west coast port. As a result of the false scent which he had been following for just over seven hours, the quarry was now 150 miles to the east of the Home Fleet flagship, but she still had nearly 1,000 miles to go to reach her destination.

Admiral Lütjens had reason to believe that at last he had evaded his pursuers but he fully realised that he would be very lucky to reach his destination without opposition. It was the German Admiral's birthday and at 1152 Admiral Raeder sent him greetings with the hope that he would 'continue to be equally successful in the coming year.' Some time later, Hitler sent him his best wishes and the Admiral took the opportunity, when thanking his flagship's company over the loud hailer system for their greetings, to remind them the worst was yet to come since it was hardly likely that the British would not strain every nerve to avenge the loss of the *Hood* and that the *Bismarck* might still be called upon to fight a life or death struggle. It appears from survivors' reports that this speech engendered deep pessimism amongst the younger members of the ship's company, who were in the majority, and it did nothing to strengthen morale.

After close consultation between the Commander-in-Chief Coastal Command, Air Chief Marshal Sir Frederick Bowhill – himself an old sailor – and the Admiralty Naval Staff, it was decided to establish during daylight on the 26th two cross-over patrols covering the approaches to the Bay of Biscay, using Catalina aircraft equipped with long-range tanks. The northern one would take care of possible enemy courses between Brest and the middle of the Bay, while the southern one covered from the middle of the Bay to Cape Finisterre. A patrol by six submarines was also established 120 miles to the west of Brest and later that evening it was moved south to take in the approaches to St. Nazaire.

During the night of 25/26 May, the weather deteriorated considerably. The wind from the north-west rose to gale force, whipping up a nasty sea which added to the difficult of high-speed steaming. The visibility was reduced from time to time by heavy rain squalls and dark clouds scudded low over the surface of the turbulent sea. Although, during the forenoon of the 25th, the Admiralty had placed the *Rodney* and the *Ramillies* under his orders, Admiral Tovey had no accurate information of their whereabouts. The former had not reported her position since that forenoon and, during the same afternoon, the latter had been withdrawn to escort the liner *Britannic* which had originally had the *Rodney* for escort. In fact, the Admiralty was now so uncertain of the position of the many isolated ships in the area of operations that since 0600/25 the sending out of situation reports had been discontinued for fear that they might be so inaccurate as to be misleading, although up to that time they had proved of great value.

So, as Admiral Tovey surveyed the situation on the gloomy and stormy morning of 25 May, it was not an encouraging picture which presented itself. Shortage of fuel had begun to cause him serious concern and at 2238 the previous evening he had felt it necessary to warn the Admiralty that he might have to reduce speed to economise fuel. He was now without a destroyer screen, as the seven ships carrying out this duty had left him to replenish in Iceland, as had also the *Prince of Wales*; the *Victorious* and the four cruisers with her, on completion of the day's search had had to follow suit and, moreover, there were no destroyers to screen the carrier. It seemed to him that everything now depended on Force H hurrying northward. The *Ark Royal*, with her experienced and fully trained air crews might prove invaluable in reducing the enemy's speed and so enable the *King George V* to overtake her and bring her to action. But the nearer the *Bismarck* came to the French coast the easier it would be for German aircraft and submarines to come to her aid and, since he was without a destroyer screen, this could be a serious menace.

Unknown to him, the previous day Group West had informed Admiral Lütjens that Focke-Wulf 200 aircraft would carry out reconnaissance as far as possible to the west and that strong air forces were available to cover the *Bismarck* when she reached longitude 14° west. Seven U-boats, later amended to five, were established on patrol 300 miles to the west of Brest. At 2230/25 Admiral Tovey had asked the Admiralty what chances there were of making some destroyers available, both for the *King George V* and the *Rodney*, for, although he knew that the latter had had three destroyers in company, he assumed that by now they would also have had to leave to refuel. The Admiralty fully appreciated Admiral Tovey's anxiety and decided to denude troop convoy WS.8B of its escort of five destroyers and send them to join the Commander-in-Chief. It was a calculated risk but, in the circumstances, fully justified as, according to the latest intelligence, there were no U-boats in the vicinity of the convoy which, at that time (midnight 25/26 May), was only 240 miles to the south-east of the *King George V*. The five destroyers were part of the 4th Destroyer flotilla commanded by the redoubtable Captain (later Admiral of the Fleet Sir Philip) Vian in the *Cossack* and it was decided to send him with *Sikh* and *Zulu* to join the *King George V*, and the *Maori* with the Polish manned destroyer *Piorun*, to join the *Rodney*. As the convoy was under the operational control of the Commander-in-Chief Western Approaches, the Admiralty told him to issue the necessary instructions and he managed to find a sixth destroyer, the *Jupiter*, exercising in the Irish Sea, which was also told to join Admiral Tovey but, of course, having a much greater distance to go, she could not arrive as soon as the other five. At 0200/26 a signal was despatched giving effect to the above movements.

To Admiral Somerville, whose Force H was now approaching the scene of operations, the re-location of the *Bismarck* was naturally uppermost in his mind but he had very little information to work on other than that she was making in the general direction of Brest. After consulting by signal with Captain Maund of the *Ark Royal*, it was decided to fly off the first air search at daylight on the 26th, orientated to cover possible enemy speeds between 25 and 21 knots. If that search were unsuccessful, another one beginning about 1300 would be launched to cover speeds down to 18 knots and, if that too failed, a third one covering speeds down to 15 knots would be flown off. There was another matter which was causing him some concern. He knew that the German battle-cruisers *Scharnhorst* and *Gneisenau* had gone into Brest after their Atlantic foray and that they had been bombed there but he was not aware if they were fit to put to sea to join forces with the *Bismarck* as, it will be recalled, was Admiral Raeder's original intention. He therefore took the opportunity at 0900 on the morning of the 26th, when he was obliged to detach his destroyers to return to Gibraltar to refuel, to order the senior officer to make two signals when 150 miles clear of the *Renown*, one addressed to the Admiralty gave his position, course and speed at 0730/26, the other addressed to the Commander-in-Chief Plymouth requested information about the most recent reconnaissance of Brest. Due to changing radio frequencies, information to the effect that both ships were still in harbour at 1930/25 did not reach him in time to prevent the launching of a security patrol at 1716/26 to search to the north and west.

The north-westerly gale which was causing the *King George V* to corkscrew uncomfortably as she steamed eastward at 24 knots with the sea on her port quarter, impeded the progress of Force H steering almost head on into it. During the night, speed had to be reduced progressively from 25 to 23, to 19 knots and finally during the middle watch (0000 to 0400) to 17 knots. Even at this speed the *Renown* was taking in green seas over her forecastle, while the *Ark Royal*'s flying deck, unceasingly swept by spray, was pitching with a rise and fall as measured by sextant at the stern of over 50 feet. In peace time, under such conditions, it would have been out of the question to attempt to operate aircraft but in war, risks have to be taken. The reduction in speed during the night had delayed the carrier's arrival at the planned point of departure for the first of the searches for the *Bismarck* and, as a compromise, Captain Maund obtained Admiral Somerville's permission to move the search area 35 miles to the south-east. This enabled launching to begin at 0830 instead of 0900. Ranging aircraft on the wet, slippery, pitching flight deck was most hazardous but it was accomplished without accident. At 0835 the ship turned into the eye of the wind and reduced speed to 10 knots so that launching could begin. One by one, the ten Swordfish aircraft detailed for the first search opened their throttles and, moving in fits and starts along the see-sawing deck, gathered flying speed and took off. Immediately six more Swordfish in the hangar, already fitted with long-range tanks, were prepared for launching, should the *Bismarck* be sighted. Meanwhile the ship herself altered course to north and headed for the rendezvous 50 miles away to which the aircraft had been ordered to return.

Chapter 5

26 May – *Bismarck* Relocated

—⚓—

But it was not to *Ark Royal*'s gallant Swordfish crews that the honour of relocating the *Bismarck* was to be accorded. Five hours before they had made their perilous take-off, at 0300/26 two Catalina aircraft of Coastal Command had set out from their base on Lough Erne in Northern Ireland to begin the cross-over patrols in the Bay of Biscay referred to above. Gradually darkness gave way to daylight and the crews were able to see below them the white-topped waves of the gale-swept ocean as they flew on hour after hour to reach their initial positions. Suddenly at 1030, when flying at a height of only 500 feet, the pilot of Catalina A of 209 Squadron, Flying Officer D.A. Briggs, on the southernmost of the two patrols, sighted the dark grey hull of a warship. Since she was alone and without destroyer escort he assumed it must be the *Bismarck* (although, unknown to him, it might equally well have been the *King George V* or *Rodney*) and he sent off a signal to this effect. The Catalina then took cover in a cloud but nine minutes later broke through right above the battleship which promptly opened fire, fortunately without scoring a hit, although the aircraft's hull was holed by a number of splinters, one of which passed between the First and Second pilots. In taking avoiding action, the Catalina temporarily lost touch but, fortunately, *Ark Royal*'s search aircraft were approaching from the south-east and half an hour later one of the Swordfish sighted the same ship which was reported as an enemy cruiser. In accordance with the standard procedure whereby any aircraft making contact with an enemy vessel is immediately joined by the one next to her, another Swordfish moved over and, on sighting the ship, reported her as a battleship.

To the senior officers at sea and to the Naval Staff at the Admiralty the most welcome news of the sighting was tempered by the doubts raised by the several aircraft regarding her identity. Was it the *Prinz Eugen* or the *Bismarck*? The similar silhouettes of the two ships had caused confusion before when they were in company, now they were separated, it was more difficult to tell them apart, especially from the air. Although the pilots of the first two Swordfish, when interrogated after their return to the carrier, could not definitely identify the ship they had sighted, the Swordfish which had relieved them soon confirmed beyond doubt that she was indeed the *Bismarck*. The position of the *Bismarck* as given in Catalina Z's sighting report (and subsequently found to have placed her 25 miles too far to the west) located her 690 miles 277° from Brest, 135 miles due south of the *King George V*, 125 miles south by west from the *Rodney*, and 112 miles west-north-west from the *Renown*. It showed that she was making good about 20 knots and at that speed by daylight on the Force. The *King George V* had insufficient speed to close within range of her during daylight that day and, for the even slower *Rodney*, it was out of the question. Only Force H was in a position to challenge the *Bismarck* during her final dash for safety, but the *Renown* alone could not take her on. It was essential that she be slowed down to allow the two battleships to catch up and this meant that she must be crippled by torpedoes launched by *Ark Royal*'s aircraft or possibly Captain Vian's destroyers.

It was evident to the Admiralty too, that only Force H stood between the *Bismarck* and her goal and knowing the fighting propensities of Admiral Somerville, at 1052 they sent him a definite order that the *Renown* was not to engage the *Bismarck* unless she was already engaged with the *King George V* or *Rodney*. He therefore concentrated all his efforts on launching an air strike against her at the earliest possible moment. Before this could be done, eight search aircraft – two having remained as shadowers – had to be landed on, refuelled and rearmed. This, in the prevailing weather, might take some time but by noon it was safely accomplished with the destruction of only one aircraft which had the misfortune to be caught in the upsurge of the after end of the flying deck, just as it was attempting to land and was severely damaged.

Force H had now crossed the *Bismarck*'s line of advance and was at noon about 50 miles to the north-east of her estimated position. Since the *Ark Royal* would have to steam into the eye of the wind both when launching and landing on aircraft, it was of the greatest important to ensure that she did not go too close to or too far away from the *Bismarck* during the operation. With the wind in the north-west the position which Admiral Somerville had taken up fulfilled all these conditions. The ground lost when head to wind could be recovered between flying off and landing on by steaming down wind at high speed and without going to close to the enemy ship on her south-easterly course. By 1415 the fifteen Swordfish aircraft detailed for the strike were ready in the hangar and the crews briefed. They were brought up on deck and at 1450 they began to take off. The Pilots and Observers had been led to expect a lone ship and, fully impressed with the great importance of their mission, they were determined to press home their attack. One aircraft developed a defect on taking off and had to be re-embarked.

During the afternoon the *Rodney* was sighted from the *King George V* converging slowly on her from the port beam and by 1800 she had taken station astern of the flagship. Asked by the Commander-in-Chief what speed he could do, Captain Dalrymple-Hamilton optimistically replied '22 knots', but this proved to be rather more than the seventeen year-old ship, badly in need of a refit, could manage. The *Rodney* still had the destroyers *Tartar* and *Mashona* in company, the *Somali* having had to be detached to replenish with fuel. Although Admiral Tovey had been hoping for the arrival of Captain Vian's flotilla, he quite expected that, on receipt of the position of the *Bismarck*, he would have decided to disregard his previous instructions and lead his destroyers towards the enemy with a view to delivering a night torpedo attack. What the Commander-in-Chief was anxiously awaiting was the result of the strike by *Ark Royal*'s aircraft. Little did he know what mischance had attended it.

To reinforce the two shadowing Swordfish aircraft, and in view of the adverse state of the weather, at 1315 Admiral Somerville had ordered the cruiser *Sheffield* to proceed ahead and establish contact with the *Bismarck*. Unfortunately, the message, being transmitted visually, was not received by the *Ark Royal* who, preoccupied with the operation of aircraft, did not see the departure of the *Sheffield* in the prevailing poor visibility. The Admiral followed up his plain language signal to the *Sheffield* with an encrypted one, addressed to the Admiralty and repeated to the *Ark Royal*, stating what he had done but, owing to the large number of messages being received at that time, especially those from the shadowing aircraft, and the fact that it was only repeated for information, there was some delay in decoding it. It was not, therefore, shown to Captain Maund until more than an hour after the strike had been launched and, when he read it, he at once realised the disastrous consequences which might result from this lack of information. He immediately sent off a signal in plain language to the Striking Force 'Look out for *Sheffield*' but, alas, it was too late.

The *Sheffield* was aware of the despatch of the Striking Force and it was, therefore, no surprise to Captain Larcom, her commanding officer when, at about 1545, he sighted it and a warning went out to the A/A gun positions that friendly aircraft were approaching. The *Sheffield* was at the time about 20 miles to the north of the *Bismarck* but not yet in touch with her. Suddenly, to everyone's amazement, they noticed that the aircraft had broken formation and were diving to the attack. Captain Larcom went on to full speed and put his helm hard over to confuse their aim but a further surprise was in store. The warheads of half the torpedoes released exploded on hitting the water or in the wake, so that he only had to avoid the six or seven which did not explode and this he successfully managed to do. Moreover, as a result of good fire discipline, not a shot had been fired.

When Admiral Tovey received Admiral Somerville's report of the result of the air strike, which tersely announced 'No hits' he felt that the scales were now tilted very much in favour of the *Bismarck*. Even when he received the amplifying news that another strike would take off at 1830, the failure of the first one, about which he had as yet received no details, did not augur well for the success of the second, which he appreciated would be the last one that day. There were still Captain Vian's destroyers and he knew that under his forceful leadership the attacks would be pressed well home; yet a single ship with complete freedom of manoeuvre was not an easy target and the prevailing weather could not have been more unfavourable for destroyer night torpedo attacks. Fuel in the *King George V* was now down to 32 per cent remaining and the *Rodney* had only enough to allow her to remain until 0800/27, so the unpleasant fact had to be faced that, unless there was a favourable change in the situation during the night, he would be obliged to abandon the chase. After four days and nights of pursuit covering over 2,000 miles, it was a heart-breaking situation with which to be confronted.

A dispirited group of airmen returned to the *Ark Royal*, but Captain Maund soon restored their morale. He exonerated them from all blame for the mistake and told them they would have another opportunity to strike at the *Bismarck* as soon as their aircraft had been re-armed and re-fuelled. Further, that the obviously defective Duplex pistols fitted to the torpedoes would be replaced by contact ones set to run at 22 feet. Meanwhile, at 1740, the *Sheffield* had sighted the *Bismarck* and taken station ten miles astern of her from which position she was able to shadow her closely. *Ark Royal*'s second striking force, consisting of fifteen Swordfish, took off at 1910 and formed up in two squadrons of three sub-flights. The *Sheffield* had reported the enemy as bearing 167° distant 38 miles from the carrier and the aircraft had been ordered to get in touch with the cruiser so that she could use her D/F equipment to guide them to their target. As they neared the *Bismarck* they entered a bank of thick cloud, the base of which was only about 700 feet from the water. While climbing through it the force became split up, but at 2047 number one sub-flight of three aircraft to which one of number three sub-flight had attached itself, dived through the cloud to sight the *Bismarck* about four miles away down wind. They manoeuvred to approach her from the port beam and, under intense and accurate fire, released their torpedoes, one of which was seen to have hit. During the next forty minutes the remaining aircraft, some of which came upon the enemy from an unexpected direction and had either to work round or take cloud cover before making a fresh approach, made their attacks. The flak was intense and, to the Germans, it seemed that it was only the flimsy canvas structure of the aircraft through which the A/A shells tore without detonating that saved them from complete destruction. Altogether thirteen torpedoes were fired, two having been jettisoned, and two hits and one probable hit were claimed. All the aircraft returned safely, though five had been damaged by gunfire and the pilot and gunner of one of them were wounded; one aircraft crash landed.

The real extent of the damage inflicted on the *Bismarck* was not at first apparent to the British forces. Lieutenant Commander Gerhard Junack, an engineer officer and survivor from the *Bismarck*, describes it as follows:

> 'One torpedo which hit amidships caused no damage, but the second affected the rudders disastrously by jamming the portside rudder at a 15° angle. Immediately, the *Bismarck* became no longer manoeuvrable. The torpedo hit on the rudder shook the ship so badly that even in my zone of action in the turbine room the deck

plates were thrown in the air and the hull vibrated violently... The stern compartments in the ship were now flooding, but the men who had been stationed there could still be saved and soon the carpenters and repair crew came through making their way aft ... eventually it was found possible to connect the hand rudder. But the old rudder would not budge and to attempt to cut it away with underwater saws was quite impossible because of the heavy swell. A proposal to force the rudder out from below with the help of explosives was rejected because of the proximity to the propellers.'[11]

Admiral Lütjens seems quickly to have reached the conclusion that there was now little chance of saving the ship from the fate that he was certain would sooner or later overtake her. At 2140 he signalled Group West 'Ship no longer manoeuvrable – we fight to the last shell – Long live the Führer.'

The *Sheffield* was the first to appreciate that something serious was amiss when she noticed that the *Bismarck* had veered round to port and she found herself under fire from her 15in guns. Six accurate salvoes were discharged and, although no hits were obtained, splinters from a near miss killed three men and wounded two others stationed at the anti-aircraft guns. The Cruiser made smoke and turned away at high speed and, as she did so, Captain Vian's destroyers were observed approaching from the westward and they were directed on to their target. At 2136 Captain Larcom reported that the *Bismarck* appeared to be steering 340° and four minutes later he amended it to North then at about 2155 he lost touch and continued on what he believed was a parallel course to the stricken ship.

Admiral Tovey received the *Sheffield*'s reports of the *Bismarck*'s course with a certain amount of reserve but, at 2142, he altered course to south and steered towards her position with a view to making contact from the eastward. When, however, at 2228 he received a signal from Admiral Somerville reporting that *Ark Royal*'s second strike had achieved a hit, followed twelve minutes later by a claim to have made a possible second one, he decided in view of the gathering darkness and the uncertain prospects of interception under favourable conditions, to defer engagement until dawn. To that end, at 2306 he altered course to the eastward and northward to work his way around the *Bismarck* so as to approach her from the west when she would be silhouetted against the eastern horizon.

As Captain Vian, with his five destroyers spread two and a half miles apart on a line of bearing 070°-250°, swept downwind on a south-easterly course of 120° towards his target, he hoped to contact her ahead of his own ship, the *Cossack* but, instead, the Polish destroyer *Piorun* on his port wing was the first to sight her. At 2228 she reported the *Bismarck* bearing 145° distant 9 miles. He had decided that now that the battleship was apparently disabled, his first duty was to shadow her and in every way assist the Commander-in-Chief in bringing her to action with his two battleships. At the same time, he hoped that there would be opportunities for delivering torpedo attacks on her, which would cripple her still further, provided these did not involve heavy losses to his ships. At 2248, therefore, he ordered his ships to take up shadowing positions all round the *Bismarck*. It took a little time for some of the destroyers to work round to their positions without going too close to their still very formidable opponent. The *Piorun* quickly discovered the need for caution when, at a range of 13,500 yards, she engaged her much larger opponent and received in reply three salvoes of 15in shells one of which straddled her. As darkness fell the weather appeared to deteriorate and the heavy rain squalls became more frequent, conditions which did not favour a synchronised torpedo attack. Nevertheless, at 2324 Vian ordered his ships to take up stations for the delivery of one, but soon afterwards, realising how adverse the circumstances were, he cancelled the order and told them to attack independently.

Meanwhile, on board the *Bismarck* all hope of freeing the damaged rudder appears to have been abandoned. At 2358 Admiral Lütjens despatched another heroic signal, this time addressed to Hitler, 'We fight to the last in our belief in you my Führer, and in the firm faith of Germany's victory', to which Hitler duly replied and, in a message to the crew, promised: 'What can still be done, will be done'; but, apart from ordering all U-boats in the area to concentrate round her, whether they had torpedoes or not, and having tugs stand by in case there should be a favourable change in the situation, little else was possible. She was still too far out for effective air support, the *Scharnhorst* and the *Gneisenau* were unfit for sea and the weather was too bad for destroyers of the much smaller type available. From 2300 onwards the *Bismarck* headed at slow speed into the wind, using her engines from time to time to alter course so as to open 'A' arcs or to avoid the torpedoes aimed at her by the destroyers, as first one, then another and occasionally in pairs, they closed in to deliver their attacks. Darkness, usually the cloak under which such attacks are made, now advantaged them not at all. The *Bismarck* greeted every attempt with accurately placed salvoes of both large and small calibre shell. At 2342 Captain Vian's ship, *Cossack*, was subjected to this treatment while still 8,000 yards away and splinters removed some of her radio aerials. The *Zulu* had a similar experience some eight minutes later, being straddled by three 15in salvoes; splinters from which wounded one officer and two ratings. The *Sikh* was shadowing from astern when, at 0020, the *Bismarck* made a large alteration of course to port and opened fire on her, the shell splashes preventing the Torpedo control officer from taking aim, so she had to withdraw without attacking. The *Maori*, close on the *Sikh*'s port beam, endeavoured to take over her shadowing duty but the battleship again swung round and, for a time, succeeded in throwing off all the shadowing destroyers.

At 0100 the *Zulu* steering westward re-sighted the *Bismarck* right ahead so she increased to 25 knots and, zigzagging to hinder her aim, ran up on her port quarter unobserved and at 0121 fired two torpedoes at a range of 5,000 yards, immediately coming under heavy fire from the enemy who, during the approach, had swung round from north-west to north-east and so the torpedoes missed. It was now the *Maori*'s turn. Her Captain, Commander H.T. Armstrong DSC, RN, an officer of great experience and intrepidity, observing that the enemy ship was now heading 040° crept up on her port quarter to within 4,000 yards and apparently undetected. When he reached her beam he fired a star shell in order the better to illuminate her and noticed that she was turning to starboard so, at 0137, he fired two torpedoes one of which he believed was a hit. He then manoeuvred to deliver another attack from the starboard bow, but the *Bismarck* had by now opened a very heavy fire with her main, secondary and close-range weapons, so he was obliged to withdraw at full speed and although the enemy's fire followed him out to 10,000 yards, providentially his ship escaped damage. Three minutes after the *Maori*'s attack Captain Vian, who had been creeping up on the battleship from the north-east, fired three torpedoes at her from a range of 6,000 yards. The target was plainly silhouetted in the flashes of her guns as she engaged the retiring *Maori*, and one certain torpedo hit was observed. Possibly, as a result of these hits, the *Bismarck* appears to have stopped and was so reported by the *Zulu* at 0148. The *Sikh*, which at this time was closing in from the southward, decided to try and carry out an unseen attack. At 0218, her Captain, Commander G.H. Stokes RN, having verified from his radar plot that the battleship was indeed stopped, fired four torpedoes from a range of 7,000 yards and one hit was believed to have been made. Therefore, he managed to keep in touch with the enemy until 0359.

Although the destroyers were making full and frequent reports of the *Bismarck*'s position and movements, they were not in sight of the Commander-in-Chief who was naturally anxious that any difference in reckoning between them and his flagship, HMS *King George V*, should be reconciled before contact was made so, at 0236, he ordered them to fire star shell at half-hourly intervals but the frequent rain squalls often obscured them and the firing ships attracted so much attention from the enemy that Captain Vian had to order them to desist.

At about 0240 it appears that the *Bismarck* again got under way and proceeded slowly in a north-westerly direction. At 0225 the *Cossack* managed to deliver another attack on her with her one remaining torpedo at a range of 4,000 yards but no hit was claimed and she came under heavy fire, so she withdrew to the northward under smoke and subsequently altered to the west.

Once again, at 0400, touch with the *Bismarck* was temporarily lost but her position was by now known and her movements were so obviously restricted that regaining contact did not present any great problem. The position of the destroyers relative to her at this time was:

'*Cossack* to the west-north-west, *Sikh*, *Zulu*, *Maori* and *Piorun* spread in the sector covering south-east to south-west and all were now moving in to regain touch.'

In the event, this does not appear to have been achieved until just before 0600. An hour previously Captain Vian had reluctantly detached the *Piorun* to return to Plymouth for fuel. Her Captain, Commander Plawski, was eager to launch a torpedo attack but dawn was breaking so it would have been an unnecessary risk to his ship and ship's company to have attempted one in the light.

At 0550 the *Maori* re-sighted the *Bismarck* steering a mean course of 340° at 7 knots and at 0625 she illuminated her with star shell just as she emerged from a rain squall into full view of the *Sikh* who, however, escaped without being engaged. Twenty minutes later the *Maori* fired two torpedoes at a range of about 9,000 yards both of which missed but the *Bismarck* opened fire on her so she went on to 28 knots and withdrew without being hit. This was the last of the destroyer torpedo attacks and, taking into account the bad weather, the way in which they had clung to the *Bismarck* and harassed her with torpedo fire without themselves suffering damage, although coming repeatedly under intense gunfire, was described the Commander-in-Chief as 'a model of its kind'. The question of how many torpedo hits were obtained during these attacks will never be known with absolute certainty. The German account based mainly on survivors' stories, infers that none was obtained and, considering that the *Bismarck* was constantly changing course and speed, it would not be in the least surprising if that were the case. The destroyers now took up positions all round the damaged German battleship from which they could watch and report her movements and so deliver her at the appointed time to the approaching British battleships.

Chapter 6

The Final Phase

—ॐ—

As dawn broke on the morning of 27 May, the avenging forces summoned by the Admiralty from far and wide were closing in for the final reckoning with the damaged but still formidable *Bismarck*. To the northward of her were the Commander-in-Chief with the *King George V* and *Rodney*, shortly to be joined by Rear Admiral Wake-Walker in the *Norfolk*, whom we last heard of complying with Admiral Tovey's order to search to the eastward, but who, since the enemy's relocation, had been steering to the south-eastward first at 27 knots and later at 30 knots. When he intercepted the report of *Ark Royal*'s aircraft success in torpedoing the *Bismarck*, he altered course more to the southward and steered in the direction indicated by the flashes of star shell fired by the destroyers. His intention was to reach a position to the northward of the enemy from which he would be able to spot the fall of shot of the two battleships. He sighted the *Bismarck* at 0753/27, 9 miles away on a bearing of 145° and a quarter of an hour later the *King George V* loomed up 12 miles away to the southward so he was able to establish a visual link between them. Another 8in gun cruiser, the *Dorsetshire*, was escorting a homeward bound convoy from Sierra Leone when she intercepted the Catalina's sighting report of 1056/26. She was then some 360 miles south of the *Bismarck*, but, leaving the auxiliary cruiser *Bulolo* in charge of the convoy, she shaped course at high speed to the northward. She soon ran into the area swept by the north-westerly gale and was obliged to reduce speed to 25 knots and later to 20 knots. At 0833/27 she sighted the *Cossack* ahead to whom she identified herself and who gave her the bearing and distance of the *Bismarck* as 290° 6 miles. She had reached the scene of action just in time, having covered 600 miles since leaving her convoy.

Admiral Somerville, who had instructed the *Ark Royal* to be ready to carry out a dawn air strike on the *Bismarck* with twelve Swordfish aircraft, had turned south at 0115/27 and a quarter of an hour later the Commander-in-Chief instructed him to keep Force H not less than 20 miles south of the *Bismarck* so as to give the battleships a clear line of approach. At 0509 while it was still dark, an aircraft was flown off from *Ark Royal* to spot for the *King George V*'s guns, but in the gale force wind and cloud-laden sky, it failed to locate the *Bismarck* and was obliged to return. The dawn attack was also cancelled on account of the poor visibility since, with so many ships around, he was anxious that there should be no repetition of the *Sheffield* incident which, but for good luck, might well have proved disastrous. At 0810, after receiving a report from the *Maori* which had been sighted to the northward, that the *Bismarck* was only 11 miles away from her and therefore 17 from the *Renown*, Admiral Somerville ordered his force to steer south-west to open its distance from the enemy.

Action

Although the north-westerly gale was blowing with undiminished force, the light was good and the horizon clear to the north-eastward as seen from the bridge of the *King George V*. Admiral Tovey decided that, in the circumstances, the weather gauge had distinct advantages, so he planned to approach the *Bismarck* from the west-north-west and if the enemy continued to head in that direction, to deploy to the southward and engage on opposite courses at about 15,000 yards.

Between 0600 and 0700 on that fateful morning, the destroyer *Maori* acting as a link between the *King George V* and the *Bismarck*, prior to the arrival of the *Norfolk*, enabled the British battleship to obtain an accurate plot of the *Bismarck*'s position, course and speed which was of the greatest help in deciding on the course to steer to make contact. It appeared that the *Bismarck* was more or less steady on a course of 330° and making good a speed of about 10 knots. At 0708, in contrast to the rigid formation in which Vice Admiral Holland had manoeuvred his two ships prior to action with the *Bismarck*, Admiral Tovey told the *Rodney* to assume open order (that is to increase distance to 6 cables) and to adjust her bearing as suited her best. At 0737 the *King George V* led round to a course of 080° and the *Rodney* took station 20° before her port beam. At 0820, as previously mentioned, the *Norfolk* was sighted and as she was also in sight of the *Bismarck* she was able to take over the duties of 'visual link' up till then so successfully performed by the *Maori*. During the run in the Commander-in-Chief twice made adjustments to his line of approach and at 0843 the *Bismarck* came into view almost right ahead, bearing 118° distant 25,000 yards. At the time the two British battleships were steering 110° in line abreast 8 cables apart.

The *Rodney* opened fire at 0847, followed a minute later by the *King George V*. An eye-witness in the latter ship described the event:

'There was a sort of crackling roar to port – the *Rodney* has opened fire with her 16in guns and an instant later the *King George V* lets fly with her 14in. I have my glasses on the *Bismarck*. She fires all four guns from her two forward turrets, four thin orange flames. The Germans have a reputation for hitting with their early salvos. Now I know what suspended animation means. It seems to take about two hours for those shots to fall!! The splashes shoot up opposite but beyond the *Rodney*'s fo'c'sle.'[12]

The *Bismarck* opened fire at 0850 and while her first salvo fell short, with her third and fourth she straddled the *Rodney* which, having freedom of manoeuvre, was able to take avoiding action by steering towards where the last salvo had fallen knowing that a range correction would be applied to the next one which would, therefore, miss. At 0854 the *Norfolk* joined in the action with her 8in guns from her position on the enemy's starboard bow at a range of about 22,000 yards. Five minutes later, when the range was down to 16,000 yards, the *King George V* swung round to starboard to open her 'A' arcs. The *Rodney*, which had been steering an opening course from the flagship, conformed a few minutes later but by now the distance between them was about 2½ miles. With the wind on the starboard quarter there was considerable interference from cordite smoke and funnel gases so that spotting the fall of shot became very difficult. The problem was overcome to some extent with the help of radar. Soon after the *King George V* turned south, the *Bismarck* turned north and shifted her fire to her, and it became an engagement on opposite courses. The eye-witness onboard the *King George V* comments:

'The *Bismarck* turned north, steaming about 12 or 14 knots. We kept turning in and out to confuse the enemy range-takers, all the while closing the range rapidly. The Admiral kept on saying 'Close the range; get closer, get close – I can't see enough hits' and so we closed the range.'[13]

At 0902 a shell or shells from the *Rodney* were seen to hit the *Bismarck* forward and it appeared that her forward turrets had been put out of action. This is supported by Lieutenant Commander Junack who wrote:

> 'Shortly after the battle commenced a shell hit the combat mast and the fire control post in the foremast broke away. At 0902 both forward heavy gun turrets were put out of action. A further hit wrecked the forward control post, the rear control post was wrecked soon after – and that was the end of the fighting instruments.'[14]

At 0904 the *Dorsetshire* on the *Bismarck*'s starboard quarter opened fire at a range of 20,000 yards so she was now under attack from all sides. The number of shell splashes falling around her increased the difficulty of observing the fall of shot, and after nine minutes the *Dorsetshire* checked fire. The range between the *King George V* and the *Bismarck* was now steady at about 12,000 yards and at 0905 the former's secondary battery of 5.25in guns opened fire, but they added to the interferences caused by cordite smoke and after two or three minutes they were ordered to cease fire. Meanwhile, the *Rodney* fired six of her 24.5in torpedoes at the enemy at an estimated range of 11,000 yards and the *Norfolk* four 21in torpedoes at an estimated range of 16,000 yards, but none of them scored a hit.

The *Bismarck*'s bearing from both the *King George V* and the *Rodney* was drawing rapidly aft, and at 0916 Captain Dalrymple-Hamilton turned his ship 180° to starboard, but when the turn was completed he was only 8,600 yards from the enemy and at that range the effect of his 16in guns was truly devastating. The *King George V* did not turn until nine minutes later and Captain Patterson turned 150° to port, which put him 12,000 yards from the *Bismarck*. The *King George V* was having a difficult time. As she was to leeward her view of the target was obscured by smoke and the splashes of the *Rodney*'s shells and her gunnery radar set had temporarily broken down. Further, her 14in gun turrets were suffering from the same kind of mechanical defects, which had afflicted those in the *Prince of Wales*. One of them was out of action for half an hour and two others for shorter periods, so that for seven minutes her fire power was reduced by 80 per cent and for twenty-three minutes by 40 per cent and this, in less favourable circumstances, might have had very serious consequences. At 1005 she closed on the *Bismarck* to about 3,000 yards and fired several salvoes at this point blank range, then she resumed her northerly course.

The *Bismarck*'s after guns, now firing in local control, shifted their fire from the *King George V* to the *Rodney* and several shots fell close, one damaging the sluice door of her starboard underwater torpedo tube into which a torpedo had just been loaded. The turn to the north and into the wind had cleared the range and it was now possible to see the damage being inflicted on the *Bismarck*. The same eye-witness has recorded:

> 'About this time, the coppery glow of our secondary armament shells striking the armoured upper works became more and more frequent, and one fierce flame shot up from the base of the bridge structure, enveloping it as high as and including the spotting top for a flickering second.'[15]

About this time the *Bismarck* appeared to slow down and the *Rodney* began to overhaul her. Zigzagging across her bows she continued to pour a shattering fire into the blazing and battered hull of the German ship. She fired another four torpedoes at her, but again without success. Most of the *Bismarck*'s guns had been silenced, only the after superimposed turret and a few of the secondary armament guns remained in action, but by 1010 even these had fallen silent. The *Bismarck* had fought a gallant fight but the odds against her were too great. Lieutenant Commander Junack takes up the story:

> 'Gradually the noise of combat became more irregular until it sank, to become nothing more than a series of sporadic crashes; even the control bells from the bridge stopped ringing. All three turbine rooms were filled with smoke from the boiler room; fortunately no shells had yet come through the plating protecting the engine room or the electric generators... Somewhere about 1015 hours I received an order over the telephone from the Chief Engineer: 'Prepare the ship for sinking.' That was the last order I received on *Bismarck*. After that all transmission of orders collapsed.'[16]

Other survivors have told of the fearful damage within the ship. Hatches and doors wrenched from their hinges littered the decks. The red glow of fires illumined the darkened passages and thick smoke and fumes from bursting shells poisoned the atmosphere and poured from great holes six feet wide blasted in the upper deck. Listing to port and wallowing in the trough of the Atlantic swell, the once pride of the

German Navy was now a black and burning hulk. But despite the terrible battering she had received, the *Bismarck* did not sink, much to Admiral Tovey's surprise. It seemed clear that further gunfire would not hasten her end, and both his ships being extremely short of fuel, at 1015 he ordered the *King George V* and *Rodney* to break off the action and steer 027°. At 1036 he directed the *Dorsetshire* to finish her off with torpedoes, but meanwhile the fuses of the scuttling charges had been lit. At 1010 the *Norfolk*, after waiting for the *King George V* and the *Rodney* to move out of range, fired four torpedoes at a range of 4,000 yards and although she claimed two hits it does not appear that any were obtained. Ten minutes later the *Dorsetshire*, approaching from the southward, fired two torpedoes one of which exploded under the bridge on the starboard side and the other further aft. She then circled round the *Bismarck*'s bows and at 1036 fired another torpedo from a range of 2,600 yards into her port side, after which the great ship heeled over to port and started to sink by the stern; then she turned over and at 1040 disappeared from view.

There has been a great deal of discussion on the subject of whether the *Bismarck* sank as the result of the torpedo hits she had received, or the firing of the scuttling charges, or a combination of both. In the light of our present knowledge it seems reasonable to discount all the claims of torpedo hits other than those listed below, which show that she received six hits, three from 18in aircraft torpedoes and three from 21in torpedoes, viz: *Victorious*'s aircraft, one starboard side, *Ark Royal*'s aircraft, one port side and one starboard side aft, *Dorsetshire* two starboard side and one port side. Except for the vital hit that damaged the rudder, it is quite possible that the other 18in torpedoes did little damage, if any. So only the effect of the *Dorsetshire*'s three torpedoes is in question. Herr Brennecke, who has clearly made a very detailed study of the subject has this to say:

> 'Did the battleship sink as a result of the torpedo hits or on account of the scuttling charges? According to the report of the *Dorsetshire* the first two torpedoes which hit the starboard side of the *Bismarck* from close range had no visible effect. A further torpedo which was fired by the heavy cruiser against the port side was said to have caused the end. Contrary to this are the reports of eye-witnesses who did not see any results of the torpedo hits when the ship overturned. In fact the expert and responsible shipbuilder of the *Bismarck* class says that the torpedo bulkheads were strong

enough to withstand the impact of several torpedo hits. It is, however, possible in the case of the third torpedo that the water which had entered the lower compartments in the meantime as a result of the scuttling, so lessened the stability of the hull and of the torpedo protection devices that the *Bismarck* sank.'

He goes on to say:

'The question whether the heavily damaged battleship would have sunk without the scuttling charges and only on account of the torpedo hits cannot be positively answered. More probable, though not wholly provable, is the other theory that the torpedo hits had absolutely no effect and that the end of the Bismarck was entirely due to the scuttling measures undertaken.'[17]

It is difficult to believe that a torpedo exploding against the hull of a ship, even one as well built as was the *Bismarck*, would have no visible effect even though it might not injure the ship's watertight integrity, but in view of the fact that the *Dorsetshire*'s third and last torpedo was not fired until about fifteen minutes after the scuttling charges had been blown, it seems highly probable that the effect of this explosion on the already sinking ship was to hasten her end.

In his despatch on the action, Admiral Tovey paid a fitting tribute:

'The *Bismarck* had put up a most gallant fight against impossible odds, worthy of the old days of the Imperial German Navy, and she went down with her colours flying.'[18]

Since the *Dorsetshire* was the nearest to the scene of the sinking, she signalled one of *Ark Royal*'s aircraft circling round to carry out an anti-submarine patrol round her while she stopped to rescue survivors in which task she was assisted by the *Maori*. The cruiser had picked up about 80 men under very difficult conditions with the ship rolling heavily in the sea and swell, when a suspicious smoky discharge was observed about two miles to leeward. Thinking it might indicate the presence of a U-boat she reluctantly got under way, leaving the *Maori* to do what she could for the remainder. Between them they rescued four officers and 110 men and later that evening submarine U-75 rescued a further three men, while the following night the German fishing vessel *Sachsenwald*, acting as a weather ship out of Bordeaux, picked up another two. The Spanish cruiser *Canarias* also hurried to the scene but found only floating corpses. Thus, out of a ship's company of some 2,400 only 119 were saved.

The anxiety about the presence of U-boats was fully justified as was subsequently discovered. U-556 had been ordered to rendezvous with the *Bismarck* and take off her war diary which, however, she did not succeed in doing. A month later she was sunk and it was learned from survivors that at 2100 on 26 May she had found herself within range of the *Renown* and *Ark Royal* with the latter on a steady course operating aircraft. She had, however, expended all her torpedoes and was therefore unable to attack them. The German account of the operation also says:

> 'The possibilities of supporting the *Bismarck* were limited to the determined efforts of the Air Force and the submarines available in the Biscay area. All the submarines in question, with or without torpedoes, were sent to the supposed position of the *Bismarck*.'[19]

On retiring to the northward the *King George V* and *Rodney* were joined by the *Cossack*, *Sikh* and *Zulu* and by 1600 on the following day by eleven more destroyers despatched by the Admiralty to form an anti-submarine screen for the two battleships. Although it was fully expected that the Germans would retaliate for the sinking of the *Bismarck* by mounting a heavy air attack against them whilst they remained within range of the French airfields, in the event only four aircraft succeeded in locating them, one of which attacked one of the ships on the screen, and another jettisoned its bombs when attacked by a Blenheim fighter covering the fleet. The Commander-in-Chief with his force reached Loch Ewe safely at 1230 on 29 May. Two of Captain Vian's flotilla, the *Tartar* and the *Mashona*, both of whom were very short of fuel and, as a result, had been unable to keep up with the rest of the fleet and had fallen about 100 miles astern were not so lucky. At 0955/28 they were attacked by a strong force of enemy bombers sent out to attack the battleships. The two vessels stoutly fought off their attackers and tried to dodge the bombs aimed at them, but the *Mashona* was hit and began to settle. During a lull, the *Tartar* stopped and took off her crew, but she remained under attack for the rest of the day. Later that afternoon she was joined by two destroyers detached by Admiral Tovey, and all three ships reached port safely the next day. The losses in the *Mashona* amounted to one officer and 45 men.

The Commander-in-Chief's views on the Action

Altogether five battleships, three battle-cruisers, two aircraft carriers, four heavy and seven light cruisers and twenty-one destroyers in addition to some fifty aircraft from Coastal Command were employed in the operations leading up to the sinking of the *Bismarck* in what was one of the most dramatic episodes of World War II. It provided an excellent example of the use of sea-air or maritime power in which both shore-based and sea-borne aircraft played a decisive part. The German ship's lack of air support proved her undoing, as Raeder well knew it might. In a well-deserved tribute to the British forces taking part, Admiral Sir John Tovey wrote:

> 'Although it was no more than I expected, the co-operation, skill and understanding displayed by all forces during this prolonged chase gave me the utmost satisfaction. Flag and Commanding Officers of detached units invariably took the action I would have wished, before or without receiving instructions from me. The conduct of all officers and men of the Fleet which I have the honour to command was in accordance with the tradition of the Service. Force H was handled with conspicuous skill throughout the operation by Vice Admiral Sir James F. Somerville KCB, DSO and contributed a vital share in its successful conclusion. The accuracy of the enemy information supplied by the Admiralty and the speed with which it was passed were remarkable and the balance struck between information and instructions passed to forces out of visual touch with me was ideal.'[20]

The valuable part played by Coastal Command was recognised in a message sent by the Admiralty to its Commander-in-Chief:

> 'The Admiralty wish gratefully to acknowledge the part played by the reconnaissance forces under your command which contributed in a large measure to the successful outcome of the recent operations.'

Movements of the *Prinz Eugen*

Nothing more was heard of the *Prinz Eugen* from the time she parted company with the *Bismarck* at about 1800 hours on 24 May until 4 June when she was reported to have arrived at Brest. After being detached, Captain Brinkmann's first thought was to replenish with fuel from one of the supply ships which had been provided for the purpose. He accordingly steered to make contact with the tankers *Spickern* and *Esso Hamburg* which had been stationed 400 miles west and 450 miles north-west of Fayal in the Azores, respectively. He contacted the *Spickern* at 0906 on 26 May and refuelled from her. Two reconnaissance ships, the *Gonzenheim* and the *Kota Pinang*, originally stationed 300 miles south of Cape Farewell, Greenland, had been placed at his disposal and late on 27 May he made a rendezvous with them and the following day he topped up with fuel from the *Esso Hamburg*. He intended to move further south and carry out cruiser warfare in the area to the north and west of the Cape Verde Islands but on the 29th, his Chief Engineer informed him that an inspection of the main engines indicated that an extensive overhaul was necessary, so he abandoned his plan and decided to make for Brest at his best speed, reaching there on 1 June having covered 7,000 miles at an average speed of 24 knots. Her arrival marked the end of Operation Rheinübung and with it all hopes of the use of German surface ships in the war against shipping. Raeder records:

'The loss of the *Bismarck* had a decisive effect on the conduct of the war at sea. Hitler's attitude to my proposals now changed too. Up to then he had left me more or less a free hand... But now he became much more critical and more inclined to insist on his own views than before... Now his instructions to me circumscribed my use of such heavy units.'[21]

On the debit side too had to be added the loss of all the supply ships and reconnaissance vessels supporting the operation. By the middle of June they had all either been scuttled or were sunk by ships of the British fleet.

PART II

Appendix I

List of Flags and Commanding Officers and Ships Taking Part in Operations Against the *Bismarck*

—⁓—

Name of ship	Type	Flag and/or Commanding Officer	Initial disposition
King George V	B	Flag of Admiral Sir John Tovey Commander-in-Chief, Home Fleet Captain W.R. Patterson CVO, RN	Scapa
Rodney	B	Captain F.H.G. Dalrymple-Hamilton RN	At sea
Repulse	BC	Captain W.C. Tennant CB, CVO, RN	Clyde
Hood	BC	Flag of Vice Admiral L.E. Holland CB Captain R. Kerr CBE, RN	Scapa
Prince of Wales	B	Captain J.C. Leach MVO, RN	Scapa
Victorious	AC	Captain H.C. Bovell RN	Scapa
Norfolk	C	Flag of Rear Admiral W.F. Wake-Walker CB Captain A.J.L. Phillips RN	Denmark straits
Suffolk	C	Captain R.M. Ellis RN	Denmark straits
Galatea	C	Flag of Rear Admiral A.T.B. Curteis CB Captain E.W.B. Sim RN	Scapa
Aurora	C	Captain W.G. Agnew RN	Scapa
Kenya	C	Captain M.M. Denny CB, RN	Scapa
Neptune	C	Captain R.C. O'Conor RN	Scapa

Name of ship	Type	Flag and/or Commanding Officer	Initial disposition
Arethusa	C	Captain A.C. Chapman RN	At sea
Edinburgh	C	Commodore C.M. Blackman DSO, RN	At sea
Manchester		Captain H.A. Packer RN ⎫	Iceland-
Birmingham	C	Captain A.C.G. Madden RN ⎬	Faroes Passage
Inglefield	D	Captain P. Todd DSO, RN	Scapa
Active	D	Lieut. Commander M.W. Tomkinson RN	Scapa
Antelope	D	Lieut. Commander R.B.N. Hicks RN	Scapa
Achates	D	Lieut. Commander Viscount Jocelyn RN	Scapa
Anthony	D	Lieut. Commander J.M. Hodges RN	Scapa
Electra	D	Commander C.W. May RN	Scapa
Echo	D	Lieut. Commander C.H. de B. Newby RN	Scapa
Somali	D	Captain C. Caslon RN ⎫	At sea with
Tartar	D	Commander L.P. Skipwith RN ⎬	HMS
Mashona	D	Commander W.H. Selby RN ⎭	*Rodney*
Eskimo	D	Lieutenant J.V. Wilkinson RN	
Punjabi	D	Commander S.A. Buss MVO, RN	Scapa
Intrepid	D	Commander R.C. Gordon DSO, RN	Scapa
Icarus	D	Lieut. Commander D.C. Maud DSC, RN	Scapa
Nestor	D	Commander C.B. Alers-Hankey DSC, RN	Scapa
Jupiter	D	Lieut. Commander N.V.J.T. Thew RN	Londonderry

Western Approaches Command

Name of ship	Type	Flag and/or Commanding Officer	Initial disposition
Hermione	C	Captain G.N. Oliver RN	Scapa
Lance	D	Lieut. Commander R.W.F. Northcott RN	Scapa
Legion	D	Commander R.F. Jessel RN	Clyde as
Saguenay	D	Command G.R. Miles RCN	Escort for HMS
Assiniboine	D	Commodore G.C. Jones RCN	*Repulse*
Columbia	D	Lieut. Commander S.W. Davis RN	Londonderry

Plymouth Command

Name of ship	Type	Flag and/or Commanding Officer	Initial disposition
Cossack	D	Captain P.L. Vian DSO, RN	Clyde as
Sikh	D	Commander G.H. Stokes RN	escort
Zulu	D	Commander H.R. Graham DSO, RN	for Convoy WS.8B
Maori	D	Commander H.T. Armstrong DSC, RN	
Piorun	D	Commander E. Plawski, Polish Navy	

Nore Command

Name of ship	Type	Flag and/or Commanding Officer	Initial disposition
Windsor	D	Lieut. Commander Hon. J.M.G. Waldegrave DSC, RN	Scapa

Force H

Name of ship	Type	Flag and/or Commanding Officer	Initial disposition
Renown	BC	Flag of Vice Admiral Sir James F. Somerville KCB, DSO Captain R.R. McGrigor RN	Gibraltar
Ark Royal	AC	Captain L.E. Maund, RN	Gibraltar
Sheffield	C	Captain C.A.A. Larcom RN	Gibraltar
Faulknor	D	Captain A.F. de Salis RN	Gibraltar
Foresight	D	Commander J.S.C. Salter RN	Gibraltar
Forester	D	Lieut. Commander E.B. Tancock RN	Gibraltar
Foxhound	D	Commander G.H. Peters DSC, RN	Gibraltar
Fury	D	Lieut. Commander T.C. Robinson RN	Gibraltar
Hesperus	D	Lieut. Commander A.A. Tait RN	Gibraltar

America and West Indies Command

Name of ship	Type	Flag and/or Commanding Officer	Initial disposition
Ramillies	B	Captain A.D. Read RN	At sea
Revenge	B	Captain E.R. Archer RN	Halifax NS

South Atlantic Command

Name of ship	Type	Flag and/or Commanding Officer	Initial disposition
Dorsetshire	C	Captain B.C.S. Martin RN	At sea

Submarines

Name of ship	Type	Flag and/or Commanding Officer	Initial disposition
Minerve	S/M	Lieut. de Vaisseau P.M. Sommerville FFN	On patrol off SW Norway
P31	S/M	Lieut. J.B. de B. Kershaw RN	Scapa
Sealion	S/M	Commander B. Bryant DSC, RN	
Seawolf	S/M	Lieut. P.L. Field RN	English
Sturgeon	S/M	Lieut. Commander D. St Clair Ford RN	Channel
Pandora	S/M	Lieut. Commander J.W. Linton RN	On passage Gibraltar to UK
Tigris	S/M	Lieut. Commander H.F. Bone DSO, DSC, RN	Clyde
H44	S/M	Lieut. W.N.R. Knox DSC, RN	Rothesay

AC = Aircraft Carrier
B   = Battleship
BC = Battle-cruiser
C   = Cruiser
D   = Destroyer
S/M = Submarine

Appendix II

Ship's Data (British)

—∿—

HMS King George V and **Prince of Wales** (Battleships)
Displacement: 38,000 tons standard, 44,460 tons full load.
Dimensions: length 700ft (213m) between perpendiculars (LBP), beam 103ft (31.4m)
Draught: 27¾ft (8.4m).
Propulsion: 8 Admiralty Type boilers. Geared turbines. 4 shafts. SHP 125000.
Speed: 29 knots.
Armament: Ten 14in (356mm) guns (4x2) and (2x1). Sixteen 5.25in (133mm) DP guns (8x2). Forty-eight 2pdr A/A guns (8x6). Sixteen 20mm single A/A guns (8x2).
Protection: 5½ (138mm) forward, 15in (381mm) abreast the magazines, 14in (356mm) abreast machinery spaces, 4½in (115mm) aft. 14in turrets – 16in (406mm) face, 15in (381mm) sides, 9in (229mm) roof, 5.25in (133mm) turrets – 6in (152mm). Director Control tower and Barbettes 16in (406mm). Deck 1in (25mm) forward and aft, 6in (152mm) over magazines, 5in (127mm) over machinery spaces.
Radar: Type 281B – 3m set used for long range A/A warning and range finding for aircraft and main armament. Type 282 – 50cm set for close range A/A guns. Type 284 – 50cm range-finding set. Type 285 – fitted to A/A directors of 5.25in guns.
Complement: 1,640 private ship.
Builders: Vickers Armstrong – *King George V*. Cammell Laird – *Prince of Wales*.

HMS Hood (Battle-cruiser)
Displacement: 42,462 tons standard, 48,360 tons full load.
Dimensions: length 860ft (262m) overall (LOA), beam 105ft (32m)
Draught: 28½ft designed (8.6m) but in 1940 31½ft (9.5m)
Propulsion: Admiralty Type boilers. Geared turbines. 4 shafts. SHP 144000.

Speed: designed 32 knots, in 1940 29½ knots.

Armament: Eight 15in (381mm) guns (4x2). Twelve 5.5in (140mm) guns six each side. Eight 4in (100mm) A/A guns (4x2). Twenty-four 2pdr (40mm) (8x3). Four 21in (533mm) torpedoes in twin above water mountings. UP projectiles.

Protection: Main belt 5in (127mm) forward, 12in (305mm) amidships, 6in (152mm) aft, extending 9½ft (2.9m) below main deck. A strake of 7in (178mm) above the main belt reached to the upper deck, which was 1½in (37mm) thick. The main deck was 3in (76mm) thick and the lower deck 2in (51mm) thick.

Radar: There are no records to show with what radar sets the ship was equipped, but reliable sources indicate that she was fitted with Type 284 Gunnery radar only.

Complement: 1,421 as flagship.

Builders: John Brown and Co., Clydebank.

HMS Rodney (Battleship)

Displacement: 33900 tons standard.

Dimensions: length 690ft (210m) between perpendiculars, beam 106ft (32.3m)

Draught: 28½ft (8.6m)

Propulsion: Geared turbines. 2 shafts. SHP 45000.

Speed: designed 23 knots, but in 1941 about 21 knots.

Armament: Nine 16in (406mm) guns (3x3). Twelve 6in (152mm) guns (6x2). Six 4.7in (120mm) A/A guns (6x1).* Twenty-four 2pdr (40mm) A/A guns (3.8). Two 24.5in (622mm) torpedo tubes below water.

Protection: Main belt 14in (356mm) over magazines and machinery spaces. Deck 3¾ in (96mm) forward, 6¼in (165mm) over magazines and machinery. 16in turrets front and sides 16in (406mm), roof 9in (229mm). Direct or Control tower and Barbettes 16in (406mm).

Radar: Type 281 – 3m set, air warning and surface ranging. Type 284 – 50cm range-finding set.

Complement: 1,314.

Builders: Cammell Laird

HMS Ramillies and Revenge (Battleships)

Displacement: 29150 tons standard.

Dimensions: length 580ft (176m) between perpendiculars, 620½ft (189m) overall; beam 88½ft (27m) with bulges 102ft (31m)

---

* Not fitted until after the action on 26 May.

Draught: 28½ft (8.6m).
Propulsion: Turbines. 4 shafts. SHP 40000.
Speed: 21½ knots.
Armament: Eight 15in (380mm) guns (4x2). Twelve 6in (150mm) guns (12x1). Eight 4in (102mm) A/A guns (4x2). Sixteen 2pdr A/A guns (8x2). *Revenge* 2 and *Ramillies* 4 – 21in (533mm) torpedoes STT.
Protection: Main belt 4-6in (102-152mm) at ends, 6-13in (152-330mm) amidships. Deck forward, 1-2½in (25-63mm), amidships 1¾-2in (36-51mm), aft 3-5½in (76-139mm). Turret sides 13in (330mm), roof 4¼in (108mm). Conning Tower 11-13in (279-330mm).
Complement: 1,146.
Builders: Vickers Armstrong, launched 29.5.1915 - *Revenge*. Beardmore, launched 12.9.1916 - *Ramillies*.

HMS Renown (Battle-cruiser)
Displacement: 32000 tons standard.
Dimensions: length 750ft (228m) between perpendiculars, beam 103ft (31.4m).
Draught: 27ft (8.2m).
Propulsion: Geared turbines. 4 shafts. SHP 120000.
Speed: 29 knots.
Armament: Six 15in (380mm) guns (3x2). Twenty 4.5in (115mm) DP guns (10x2). Twenty-four 2pdr (40mm) A/A guns (8x3).
Protection: Main belt 4-6in (100-150mm) forward, 6-9in (150-230mm) amidships, 3in (76mm) aft. Deck 2½-3in (63-76mm) forward, 3-4in (76-102mm) amidships, 3½-4in (88-102mm) aft. Turrets 11in (280mm) sides, 9in (230mm) roof. Conning Tower 10in (254mm).
Aircraft: Two Walrus amphibians.
Complement: 1,205.
Builders: Fairfields. Reconstructed and re-engined by Cammell Laird.

HMS Repulse (Battle-cruiser)
Displacement: 32000 tons standard.
Dimensions: length 750ft (228m) between perpendiculars, beam 103ft (31.4m).
Draught: 27ft (8.2m).
Propulsion: Geared turbines. 4 shafts. SHP 120000.
Speed: 29 knots.
Armament: Six 15in (380mm) guns (3x2). Twelve 4in (102mm) guns (4x3). Eight 4in (102mm) A/A guns (2x2) and (4x1). Sixteen 2pdr (40mm) A/A guns (8x2). Eight 21in (533mm) above water torpedo tubes.
Protection: Main belt 4-6in (100-150mm) forward, 6-9in (150-230mm)

amidships, 3in (76mm) aft. Deck 2½–3in (63–76mm) forward, 3–4in (76–102mm) amidships, 3½–4in (88–102mm) aft. Turrets 11in (280mm) sides, 9in (230mm) roof, Conning Tower 10in (254mm).
Complement: 1,181.
Builders: John Brown Ltd.

HMS Victorious (Aircraft carrier)
Displacement: 26000 tons standard.
Dimensions: length 673ft (205m) between perpendiculars, 753ft (229m) overall; beam 95¾ft (29m).
Draught: 24ft (7.3m).
Propulsion: Geared turbines. 3 shafts. SHP 110000.
Speed: 32 knots.
Armament: Sixteen 4.5in (115mm) guns DP (8x2). Forty-eight 2pdr (40mm) A/A guns (8x6). Eight 20mm A/A guns (8x1).
Protection: Main belt and hangar sides 4½in (114mm). Flight deck 2½–3in (63–76mm).
Aircraft: 72.
Complement: 1,392.
Builders: Vickers Armstrong.

HMS Ark Royal (Aircraft carrier)
Displacement: 22000 tons standard.
Dimensions: length 685ft (209m) between perpendiculars, 800ft (244m) overall; beam 94¾ft (28.8m).
Draught: 22¾ft (6.9m).
Propulsion: Geared turbines. 3 shafts. SHP 102000.
Speed: 30¾ knots.
Armament: Sixteen 4½in (115mm) A/A guns (8x2). Forty-eight 2pdr A/A guns (8x6). Eight 20mm A/A guns (8x1).
Protection: Main belt 4½in (115mm). Flight deck 2½–3in (63–70mm).
Aircraft: 72.
Complement: 1,575.
Builders: Cammell Laird, launched 13.4.1937.

HMS Norfolk and Dorsetshire (Cruisers)
Displacement: 9925 tons standard.
Dimensions: length 590ft (179m) between perpendiculars, 630ft (192m) overall; beam 66ft (20m).
Draught: 17ft (5.2m).

Propulsion: Geared turbines. 4 shafts. SHP 80000.

Speed: 32 knots.

Armament: Eight 8in (203mm) guns (4x2). Eight 4in (102mm) A/A guns (4x2). Sixteen 2pdr A/A guns (8x2). Eight 21in (533mm) torpedoes AWTT.

Protection: Main belt 3-5in (76-127mm). Deck 1½-4in (38-102mm). Turrets 1½-2in (38-51mm). DCT 3in (76mm).

Complement: 710 as flagship, otherwise 679.

Builders: Fairfield, launched 12.12.1928 – *Norfolk*. Portsmouth Dockyard, launched 29.1.1929 – *Dorsetshire.*

HMS Suffolk (Cruiser)

Displacement: 9800 tons standard.

Dimensions: length 590ft (179m) between perpendiculars, 630ft (192m) overall; beam 68¼ft (20.7m).

Draught: 16¼ft (4.9m).

Propulsion: Geared turbines. 4 shafts. SHP 80000.

Speed: 31½ knots.

Armament: Eight 8in (203mm) guns (4x2). Eight 4in (102mm) A/A guns (4x2). Eight 2pdr A/A guns (4x2). Four 21in (533mm) torpedoes AWTT.

Protection: Main belt 3-5in (76-127mm). Deck 1½in (38mm). Turrets 1½-2in (38-51mm). DCT 3in (76mm).

Complement: 710 as flagship, otherwise 679.

Builders: Portsmouth Dockyard, launched 16.2.1926.

Note. Norfolk was fitted with Type 286P radar which was a 1½m set with two fixed aerials.

Suffolk was fitted with Types 279 and 284 radar, the former a 1½m air warning set with a rotative aerial, the latter a 50cm rangefinding set for main armament direction.

HMS Birmingham and Sheffield (Cruisers)

Displacement: 9100 tons standard.

Dimensions: length 591½ft (179.5m) overall, 558ft (170m) between perpendiculars, beam 61¾ft (18.8m)

Draught: 17ft (5.2m).

Propulsion: Geared turbines. 4 shafts. SHP 75000.

Speed: 32 knots.

Armament: Twelve 6in (152mm) guns (4x3). Eight 4in (102mm) A/A guns (4x2). Eight 2pdr A/A guns (4x2). Eight 40mm A/A (4x2). Six 21in (533mm) torpedoes (3x2) AWTT.

Protection: Main belt 3-4in (76-102mm). Deck 2in (51mm). Turrets 1-2in

(25.5–51mm). DCT 4in (102mm).
Aircraft: Three
Complement: 700.
Builders: Devonport Dockyard, launched 1.9.1936 – *Birmingham*. Vickers Armstrong, launched 23.7.1936 – *Sheffield*.

HMS Manchester (Cruiser)
Displacement: 9400 tons standard.
Dimensions: length 558ft (170m) between perpendiculars, 59½ft (179.5m) overall; beam 62¼ft (19m).
Draught: 17½ft (5.3m).
Propulsion: Geared turbines. 4 shafts. SHP 82500.
Speed: 32½ knots.
Armament: Twelve 6in (152mm) guns (4x3). Eight 4in (102mm) A/A guns (4x2). Eight 2pdr A/A guns (4x2). Eight 40mm A/A (4x2). Six 21in (533m) torpedoes (3x2) AWTT.
Protection: Main belt 3–4in (76–102mm). Deck 2in (51mm). Turrets 1–2in (25.5–51mm). DCT 4in (102mm).
Aircraft: Three.
Complement: 700.
Builders: Hawthorne Leslie, launched 12.4.1937.

HMS Edinburgh (Cruiser)
Displacement: 10000 tons.
Dimensions: length 579ft (176m) between perpendiculars, 613½ft (187m) overall; beam 63¼ft (19.3m)
Draught: 17¾ft (5.2m).
Propulsion: Geared turbines. 4 shafts. SHP 80000.
Speed: 32 knots.
Armament: Twelve 6in (152mm) guns (4x3). Twelve 4in (102mm) A/A guns (6x2). Sixteen 2pdr A/A guns (8x2). Six 21in (533mm) torpedoes (3x2) AWTT.
Protection: Main belt 4½in (115mm). Deck 2in (51mm). Turrets 2½ –1in (64–25mm). DCT 4in (102mm).
Aircraft: Three.
Complement: 850.
Builders: Swan Hunter, launched 31.3.1938.

HMS Arethusa, Aurora and Galatea (Cruisers)
Displacement: 5220 tons standard.

Dimensions: length 480ft (146m) between perpendiculars, 506ft (154m) overall; beam 51ft (16.2m)
Draught: 13¾ft (4m).
Propulsion: Geared turbines. 4 shafts. SHP 64000.
Speed: 32 knots.
Armament: Six 6in (152mm) guns (3x2). Eight 4in (102mm) A/A guns (4x2). Eight 2pdr A/A guns (4x2). Six 21in (533m) torpedoes (3x2) AWTT
Protection: Main belt 2in (51mm). Deck 2in (51mm). Turrets and DCT 1in (25mm).
Complement: 450.
Builders: Chatham Dockyard, launched 6.3.1934 – *Arethusa*. Portsmouth Dockyard, launched 20.8.1936 – *Aurora*. Scotts, launched 9.8.1934 – *Galatea*.

HMS Kenya (Cruiser)
Displacement: 8000 tons standard.
Dimensions: length 538ft (163.5m) between perpendiculars, 555½ft (168.5m) overall; beam 62ft (19m).
Draught: 16½ft (5m).
Propulsion: Geared turbines. 4 shafts. SHP 72500.
Speed: 33 knots.
Armament: Twelve 6in (152mm) guns (4x3). Eight 4in (102mm) A/A guns (4x2). Nine 2pdr A/A guns (4x2 and 1x1). Six 21in (533m) torpedoes (3x2) AWTT.
Protection: Main belt 3¼in (82mm). Deck and Turrets 2in (51mm). DCT 4in (102mm).
Aircraft: Three.
Complement: 730.
Builders: John Brown, launched 18.8.1939.

HMS Neptune (Cruiser)
Displacement: 7175 tons standard.
Dimensions: length 530ft (161m) between perpendiculars, 554½ft (168m) overall; beam 55¼ft (16.8m)
Draught: 16ft (4.9m).
Propulsion: Geared turbines. 4 shafts. SHP 72000.
Speed: 32½ knots.
Armament: Eight 6in (152mm) guns (4x2). Eight 4in (102mm) A/A guns (4x2). Eight 2pdr A/A guns (4x2). Eight 21in (533mm) torpedoes (4x2) AWTT.
Protection: Main belt 2-4in (51-102mm). Deck 2in (51mm). Turrets and

DCT 1in (25mm).
Aircraft: One.
Complement: 550.
Builders: Portsmouth Dockyard, launched 31.1.1933.

HMS Hermione (Cruiser)

Displacement: 5450 tons standard.
Dimensions: length 485ft (148m) between perpendiculars, 512ft (155m) overall; beam 50½ft (15.4m)
Draught: 14ft (4.3m).
Propulsion: Geared turbines. 4 shafts. SHP 62000.
Speed: 33 knots.
Armament: Ten 5.25in (133mm) DP guns (5x2). Eight 2pdr A/A guns (4x2). Six 21in (533m) torpedoes (3x2) AWTT
Protection: Main belt 2-3in (51-76mm). Deck ½-2½in (13-51mm). Turrets 1-2in (25-51mm). DCT 1in (25mm).
Complement: 550.
Builders: Stephen, launched 18.5.1936.

HMS Inglefield (Destroyer – flotilla leader)

Displacement: 1530 tons standard.
Dimensions: length 326ft (98.8m) between perpendiculars, 337ft (102.2m) overall; beam 34ft (10.3m)
Draught: 9ft (2.7m).
Propulsion: Geared turbines. 2 shafts. SHP 38000.
Speed: 36 knots.
Armament: Five 4.7in (119mm) DP guns (5x1). Ten 21in (533mm) torpedoes (5x2) AWTT.
Complement: 175.
Builders: Cammell Laird, launched 15.10.1936.

HMS Intrepid and Icarus (Destroyers)

Displacement: 1370 tons.
Dimensions: length 321ft (94.6m) between perpendiculars, 323ft (98m) overall; beam 32¼ft (9.8m)
Draught: 8½ft (2.6m).
Propulsion: Geared turbines. 2 shafts. SHP 34000.
Speed: 36 knots.
Armament: Four 4.7in (119mm) DP guns (4x1). Ten 21in (533mm) torpedoes (5x2) AWTT.

Complement: 145.
Builders: White, launched 17.12.1936 – *Intrepid*. John Brown, launched 26.11.1936 - *Icarus*.

HMS Echo and Electra (Destroyers)
Displacement: 1375 tons standard.
Dimensions: length 318¼ft (96.5m) between perpendiculars, 329ft (100m) overall; beam 33¼ft (10m).
Draught: 8½ft (2.6m).
Propulsion: Geared turbines. 2 shafts. SHP 36000.
Speed: 35½ knots.
Armament: Four 4.7in (119mm) DP guns (4x1). Eight 21in (533mm) torpedoes (4x2) AWTT.
Builders: Denny Brothers, launched 16.2.1934 – *Echo*. Hawthorn Leslie, launched 16.2.1934 - *Electra*.

HMS Anthony, Achates, Antelope, Active and Hesperus * (Destroyers)
Displacement: 1350 tons standard.
Dimensions: length 312ft (95m) between perpendiculars, 323ft (98m) overall; beam 32¼ft (10.5m)
Draught: 8½ft (2.6m).
Propulsion: Geared turbines. 2 shafts. SHP 34000.
Speed: 35 knots.
Armament: Four 4.7in (119mm) guns (4x1). Two 2pdr A/A guns (2x1). Eight 21in (533mm) torpedoes (4x2) AWTT.
Complement: 138.
Builders: Scotts, launched 24.4.1929 – *Anthony*. J. Brown, launched 4.10.1929 – *Achates*. Hawthorn Leslie, launched, 27.7.1929 – *Antelope*. Hawthorn Leslie launched, 9.7.1929 – *Active*. Thornycroft, launched 1.8.1939 – *Hesperus*.
* ex Brazilian.

HMS Jupiter (Destroyer)
Displacement: 1690 tons standard.
Dimensions: length 339½ft (103m) between perpendiculars, 356½ft (108m) overall; beam 35¾ft (10.8m)
Draught: 9ft (2.7m)
Propulsion: Geared turbines. 2 shafts. SHP 40000.
Speed: 36 knots.
Armament: Six 4.7in (119mm) guns (3x2). Four 2pdr A/A guns (1x4). Ten

21in (533mm) torpedoes (5x2) AWTT.
Complement: 183.
Builders: Yarrow Ltd, launched 27.10.1938.

HMCS Assiniboine (Destroyer)
Displacement: 1390 tons standard.
Dimensions: length 317¾ft (96.4m) between perpendiculars, 329ft (100m) overall; beam 33ft (10m).
Draught: 8¾ft (2.4m).
Propulsion: Geared turbines. 2 shafts. SHP 36000.
Speed: 35½ knots.
Armament: Four 4.7in (119mm) guns (4x1). Two 2pdr A/A guns (2x1). Eight 21in (533mm) torpedoes (4x2) AWTT.
Complement: 175.
Builders: Whites, launched 29.10.1931

HMCS Saguenay (Destroyer)
Displacement: 1337 tons standard.
Dimensions: length 309ft (93.7m) between perpendiculars, 321¼ft (97.5m) overall; beam 32¾ft (9.8m)
Draught: 8½ft (2.6m).
Propulsion: Geared turbines. 2 shafts. SHP 32000.
Speed: 34 knots.
Armament: Four 4.7in (119mm) DP guns (4x1). Two 2pdr A/A guns (2x1). Eight 21in (533mm) torpedoes (4x2) AWTT.
Complement: 138.
Builders: Thornycroft, launched 11.7.1930.

HMCS Columbia (Destroyer)
Displacement: 1060 tons standard.
Dimensions: length 309ft (93.7m) between perpendiculars, 314¼ft (95m) overall; beam 30½ft (9.3m)
Draught: 8½ft (2.6m).
Propulsion: Geared turbines. 2 shafts. SHP 27000.
Speed: 35 knots.
Armament: Three 4in (102mm) guns (3x1). One 3in (76mm) A/A guns. Four 20mm A/A guns (4x1). Three 21in (533mm) torpedoes (3x1) AWTT. One Hedgehog A/S weapon.
Complement: 146.
Builders: Newport News USA, launched 4.7.1918.

HMS Faulknor (Destroyer – flotilla leader)
Displacement: 1475 tons standard.
Dimensions: length 332ft (101m) between perpendiculars, 343ft (104m) overall; beam 33¾ft (10m)
Draught: 8¾ft (2.6m).
Propulsion: Geared turbines. 2 shafts. SHP 38000.
Speed: 36 knots.
Armament: Five 4.7in (119mm) DP guns (5x1). Eight 21in (533mm) torpedoes (4x2) AWTT.
Complement: 175.
Builders: Yarrow Ltd, launched 12.6.1934.

HMS Foresight, Forester, Foxhound and Fury (Destroyers)
Displacement: 1375 tons.
Dimensions: length 318¼ft (96.5m) between perpendiculars, 329ft (99.8m) overall; beam 33¼ft (10m)
Draught: 8½ft (2.6m).
Propulsion: Geared turbines. 2 shafts. SHP 36000.
Speed: 35½ knots.
Armament: Four 4.7in (119mm) guns (4x1). Eight 21in (533mm) torpedoes (4x2) AWTT.
Builders: Cammell Laird, launched 29.6.1934 – *Foresight*. Whites, launched 28.6.1934 – *Forester*. J. Brown, launched 12.10.1934 – *Foxhound*. Whites, launched 19.9.1934 – *Fury*.

HMS Lance and Legion (Destroyers)
Displacement: 1920 tons standard.
Dimensions: length 345½ft (105m) between perpendiculars, 362½ft (110m) overall; beam 36¾ft (11.2m)
Draught: 10ft (3m).
Propulsion: Geared turbines. 2 shafts. SHP 48000.
Speed: 36 knots.
Armament: Eight 4in (102mm) guns (4x2). Four 2pdr A/A guns (4x1). Two 20mm A/A guns (2x1). Eight 21in (533mm) torpedoes (4x2) AWTT.
Complement: 226.
Builders: Yarrow Ltd., launched 28.11.1940 – *Lance*. Hawthorn Leslie, launched 26.12.1939 – *Legion*.

HMS Nestor and Polish Piorun (Destroyers)
Displacement: 1690 tons standard.

Dimensions: length 339½ft (103m) between perpendiculars, 356½ft (108m) overall; beam 35¾ft (11m)
Draught: 9ft (2.7m).
Propulsion: Geared turbines. 2 shafts. SHP 40000.
Speed: 36 knots.
Armament: Six 4.7in (119mm) guns (3x2). Four 2pdr A/A guns (4x1). Two 20mm A/A guns (2x1). Ten 21in (533mm) torpedoes (5x2) AWTT.
Complement: 183.
Builders: Fairfield, launched 9.7.1940 – *Nestor*. J. Brown, launched 7.5.1940 – *Piorun*.

HMS Cossack, Maori, Zulu, Sikh, Somali, Mashona, Tartar and Punjabi (Tribal class destroyers)
Displacement: 1870 tons standard.
Dimensions: length 355½ft (108m) between perpendiculars, 377½ft (114.6m) overall; beam 36½ft (11.1m).
Draught: 9ft (2.7m).
Propulsion: Geared turbines. 2 shafts. SHP 44000.
Speed: 36 knots.
Armament: Eight 4.7in (119mm) guns (4x2). Four 2pdr A/A guns (4x1). Four 21in (533mm) torpedoes (4x1) AWTT.
Complement: *Cossack, Somali, Tartar* 219, remainder 190.
Builders: Vickers Armstrong, launched 8.6.1937 and 3.9.1937 – *Cossack* and *Mashona*. Fairfield, launched 7.7.1937 – *Maori*. Stephen, launched 17.2.1937 and 23.9.1937 – *Sikh* and *Zulu*. Swan Hunter, launched 24.8.1937 and 21.10.1937 – *Somali* and *Tartar*. Scotts, launched 18.12.1937 – *Punjabi*.

HMS Windsor (Destroyer)
Displacement: 1100 tons standard.
Dimensions: length 300ft (91m) between perpendiculars, 312ft (95m) overall; beam 29½ft (9m)
Draught: 10¾ft (3.3m).
Propulsion: Geared turbines. 2 shafts. SHP 27000.
Speed: 34 knots.
Armament: Three 4.7in (119mm) guns (3x1). One 3in (76mm) A/A gun. Two 2pdr A/A guns (2x1). Four 20mm A/A guns (4x1). Three 21in (533mm) torpedoes (1x3) AWTT.
Complement: 125.
Builders: Scotts launched 21.6.1918.

Appendix III

Ship's Data (German)

—⚓—

Bismarck (Battleship)
Captain Ernst Lindemann
Displacement: 41,700 tons standard, 50,900 tons full load.
Dimensions: length 823¼ft (251m) between perpendiculars, 790½ft (241m) waterline (LWL); beam 118ft 1in (36m).
Draught: 33½ft (10.2m) forward, 28½ft (8.7m) aft.
Propulsion: 12 Wagner high pressure boilers operating at 870lb/in² (60.7kg/cm²) at a temperature of 842°F (450°C) in two boiler rooms supplying three sets of turbines driving 3 shafts developing 13800 SHP.
Speed: 30.8 knots on trials, designed 29½ knots.
Armament: Eight 15in (381mm) guns (4x2). Twelve 5.9in (150mm) guns (6x2) three each side. Sixteen 4.1in (105mm) A/A guns (8x2) four each side. Sixteen 37mm A/A guns (8x2). Sixteen 20mm A/A guns (16x1).
Protection: Main belt 12.5in (320mm) from just forward of foremost turret to just abaft the after one. It extended from the upper deck to 6½ft (2m) below the full load waterline. The upper deck was made of 2in (50mm) special steel below which was the armoured deck 4in (102mm) thick covering four-fifths of the ship's length and sloping at the sides to meet the lower edge of the main belt. The thickness of the sloping portion was increased to 4¾in (120mm). Interior anti-torpedo compartments were made of a special soft tensile steel known as Wotan-weich-Material.
Aircraft: Six Arado type 196.
Radio/Radar: Two Direction Finding sets and one search radar set.
Complement: 2,200 with Admiral's staff.
Builders: Blohm und Voss, Hamburg, launched 14.2.1939.

Prinz Eugen (Cruiser)
Captain Helmuth Brinkmann
Displacement: 16,230 tons standard, 18,400 tons full load.
Dimensions: length 655ft (199.7m) waterline (LWL), beam 71ft (21.6m)

Propulsion: Combined Diesel and Geared steam turbines. 4 shafts.

Speed: 32 knots.

Armament: Eight 8in (203mm) guns (4x2). Twelve 4.1in (105mm) A/A guns (6x2). Twelve 37mm A/A guns (6x2). Twelve 21in (533mm) torpedoes (4x3).

Protection: Main belt 5in (127mm), bridge 2in (51mm).

Aircraft: Four and one catapult.

Builders: Deschimag & Co., Germany.

Note on German Radar

In September 1935 Admiral Raeder was shown an experimental type of radar fitted in the trial ship *Welle* and early in 1939 the German Navy took delivery of its first Freya radar set which is said to have had a range of 75 miles. It was given the cover name of Dezimeter Telegraphie or S.T. Geräte, but interest seems to have been focused on the development of a tactical set and the *Graf Spee* was equipped with a short range set known as Seetakt, which employed 375 megacycles and had a range of 9 miles. According to Herr Brennecke there is some doubt regarding whether or not the *Bismarck* was fitted with a radar set, although amongst the technical details one Radio warning set is included and 'a mattress type antenna 2x6 metres on the foreside of the D.T. Geräte was observed', which would appear to indicate that she was equipped.

Appendix IV

Aircraft Data

—ᴍ—

Swordfish

Nos. 810 and 818 squadrons – HMS *Ark Royal*.

Nos. 820 and 825 squadrons – HMS *Victorious*.

825 Squadron Leader – Lieutenant-Commander Eugene Esmonde RN.

818 Squadron Leader – Lieutenant-Commander T.P. Coode RN.

Carrier-borne, torpedo-spotter-reconnaissance aircraft.

Crew – Three for reconnaissance, two for torpedo attack.

Metal structure, fabric covered.

Manufactured by Fairey Aviation Company, Hayes, Middlesex, sub-contractors Blackburn Aircraft Ltd. Brough.

Power plant: one 690hp Bristol Pegasus III M3 or 750hp Pegasus XXX.

Dimensions: Span 45ft 6in (folded 17ft 3in), length 36ft 4in, height 12ft 10in, wing area 607sq ft, weight – light, 5200lb, loaded 9250lb.

Performance: Maximum speed 139mph at 4750ft, cruising 104/129mph at 5000ft. Range 546 miles with one 1610lb torpedo.

Fulmar

No. 800Z Squadron onboard *HMS Victorious* comprised six of these aircraft. Due to excellent night reconnaissance by them the Swordfish aircraft were able to attack the *Bismarck* on the night of May 24/25. Two-seater carrier-borne fighter. All metal stressed skin construction. Manufactured by Fairey Aviation Company.

Power plant: one 1080hp Rolls-Royce Merlin VIII.

Dimensions: span 46ft 4½in, length 40ft 3in, height 14ft, wing area 342sq ft, weight loaded 9800lb.

Performance: Maximum speed 280mph, cruising 235mph, rate of climb 1200ft per minute, range 800 miles, ceiling 26000ft.

Armament: Eight fixed Browning guns some with single Vickers K gun in rear cockpit.

Entered service in June 1940.

Appendix V

Torpedoes Fired at *Bismarck*

—⚓—

Ship	Time of Attack	No. of Torpedoes Fired (Jettisoned)	Hits	Possible Hits
Victorious	2400/25	8 (1)	1	–
Ark Royal	1550/26 on HMS Sheffield 2100/26 1016/27	13 (2) Nil (15)	2 –	1 –
Cossack	0140/27 0335/27	31	1 –	–
Maori	0137/27 0656/27	22	1 –	–
Zulu	0121/27	4	–	–
Sikh	0128/27	4	–	1
Rodney	During the action on	12	1	–
Norfolk	27 May	8	–	1
Dorsetshire	1025/27	3	2	1
		Total number fired 71	8	4
		expended 92		

Ammunition Expended During the Final Action Against *Bismarck*, 27 May 1941

—〰—

Ship	16in (41cm)	14in (35.6cm)	8in (20.3cm)	6in (15.2cm)	5.2in (13.3cm)
King George V	–	339	–	–	660
Rodney	380	–	–	716	–
Norfolk	–	–	527	–	–
Dorsetshire	–	–	254	–	–
Total	380	339	781	716	660

Appendix VII

Honours and Awards

—⁓—

In the *London Gazette* of 14 October 1941, it was announced that HM the King had given orders for the following appointments and awards for distinguished serves 'in the masterly and determined action in which the *Bismarck* was destroyed':

To Admiral Sir John Tovey KCB, DSO, Commander-in-Chief, Home Fleet, a KBE.

To Rear Admiral (then Captain) F.G.H. Dalrymple-Hamilton, HMS *Rodney*, and Captain W.R. Patterson CVO, RN, *HMS King George V*, a CB.

To Rear Admiral W.F. Wake-Walker CB, Captain H.C. Bovell RN, *HMS Victorious*, Commodore 1st Class E.J.P. Brind, Chief of Staff to the C-in-C Home Fleet, and Captain L.E.H. Maund RN, *HMS Ark Royal*, a CBE.

To Rear Admiral (then Captain) P.L. Vian a Second Bar to the DSO.

Captain J.C. Leach MVO, RN, HMS *Prince of Wales* and a further ten officers were awarded a DSO, nineteen were awarded a DSC and six received an OBE. Twenty-seven ratings received the DSM, and one a BEM.

Awards to officers and men of the Fleet Air Arm for their part in the operation included three DSO's, eleven DSC's and five DSM's.

The Commanding Officer of the Sunderland aircraft which shadowed the *Bismarck* on 23 May and the pilot of the Catalina aircraft which relocated her on 26 May received the DFC.

Vice Admiral L.E. Holland CB, Captain R. Kerr CBE, RN and Lieutenant Commander E.H.F. Moultrie of HMS *Hood* received a posthumous mention in despatches, together with 33 other officers and men of the ill-fated ship.

Notes

—ᏨᏨ—

1 Winston S. Churchill, *The Second World War*, Vol. II, The Gathering Storm, p. 529.
2 J. Brennecke, Schlachtschiff *Bismarck*, p. 259 (In a letter to the author from Admiral Patzig).
3 Brennecke, *Bismarck*, p. 43
4 Raeder, *Struggle for the Sea*, p. 212
5 Brennecke, Bismarck, p. 50.
6 Raeder, *Struggle for the Sea*, p. 212
7 Brennecke, *Bismarck*, p. 71
8 HMS *Electra* by Lieutenant Commander T.J. Cain RN (rtd.) as told to A.V. Sellwood F. Muller Ltd., 1959
9 Commander (later Captain Gerhard Bidlingmaier, Federal Germany Navy, *Exploits and end of the Battleship Bismarck*, US Naval Institute Proceedings, July 1958, pp. 77-87.
10 Edward P. von der Porten, *The German Navy in World War II*, p. 156.
11 *The Last Hours of the Bismarck* by Lieutenant Commander Gerhard Junack, Purnell's History of the Second World War, Vol. 2, No. 5.
12 Quoted by F. McMurtrie in *The Cruise of the Bismarck*, p. 32.
13 McMurtrie, *Cruise of the Bismarck*.
14 Junack, *Last Hours of the Bismarck*.
15 McMurtrie, *Cruise of the Bismarck*.
16 Junack, *Last Hours of the Bismarck*.
17 Brennecke, *Bismarck*, p. 230. (Note: In 1989 Robert Ballard located the wreck of the *Bismarck*. After three expeditions and detailed surveys, his team concluded that the direct cause of sinking was due to scuttling: sabotage by members of the crew of the engine room valves.
18 *Bismarck, The Sinking of*. Supplement to the *London Gazette* No. 39098 dated 16.10.1947.
19 Fürher Naval Conferences.
20 Tovey, 'The Sinking of the *Bismarck*'. Official despatch, paras. 92 and 93, *London Gazette* No. 38098.
21 Raeder, *Struggle for the Sea*, p. 214

Acknowledgements

—⟋⟍—

The author wishes to thank all those who in one way or another have assisted in the preparation of this book, in particular to the Librarians and staffs of the Admiralty, Imperial War Museum, and Royal United Service Institute's Libraries; to Dr Jürgen Rohwer of the Bibliothek für Zeitgeschicte, Stuggart, for permission to make use of the sketches of the *Bismarck*'s movements which he prepared for the late Captain Gerhard Bidlingmaier's study *Erfolg und Ende des Schlachtschiffes Bismarck* and published in Wehrwissenschaftliche Umschau, Heft 5/59 as well as in Herr Brennecke's book, *Schlachtschiff Bismarck*; and to Mrs Erika Gillett for her translations. The photographs reproduced are by the courtesy of the Imperial War Museum.

B.B. Schofield, 1971.

Select Bibliography

—⟋⟍—

Bidlingmaier, Captain Gerhard, *Exploits and End of the Battleship Bismarck*, (*Erfolg und Ende des Schlachtschiffes Bismarck*) US Naval Institute Proceedings, July 1958

Bradford, Ernle, *The Mighty Hood*, Hodder & Stoughton, 1959

Breyer, Siegfried (1905-1970), *Schlachtschiff und Schlachtkreuzer*, Churchill, Winston, *The Second World War, Vol.2, Their Finest Hour*, Cassell & Co. Ltd, 1949.

Brennecke, Jochen, *Schlachtschiff BISMARCK*, US Naval Institute and Koehlers Verlagsgesellschaft, Hertford 1960.

The Führer Naval Conferences, HMSO

Grenfell, Captain Russell RN, *The Bismarck Episode*, Faber & Faber, 1948

The History of the Second World War, Vol. 2, Editor in Chief, Sir Basil Liddell Hart, Purnell and Sons Ltd.

McMurtrie, Francis *The Cruise of the Bismarck*, Hutchinson & Co. c.1942.

Parkes, Oscar, *British Battleships*, Seeley Service, 1966.

Raeder, Grand Admiral Erich, *Struggle for the Sea*, Wm Kimber, 1959.

Roskill, Captain S.W. RN, *The War at Sea, 1939-45, Volume I*: The Defensive, HMSO, 1st ed.,1954.

Rüge, Vice Admiral Friedrich, *Sea Warfare 1939-45*: A German Viewpoint, Cassell & Co., 1957.

Tovey, Admiral Sir John, 'The Sinking of Bismarck,' Despatch on the action, Supplement to the *London Gazette* No. 38098, 1947.

Von der Porten, Edward P., *The German Navy in World War II*, Arthur Barker, 1970.

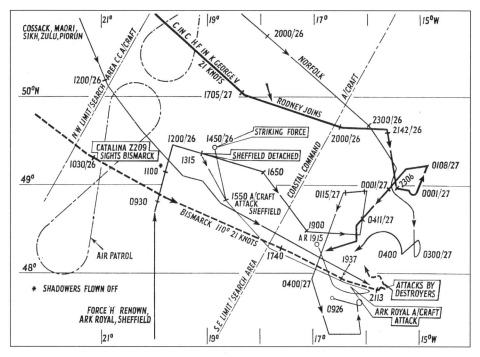

5. *Bismarck* relocated, movements of British Forces from 1030 on 26 May.

6. Final action against *Bismarck* on 27 May.

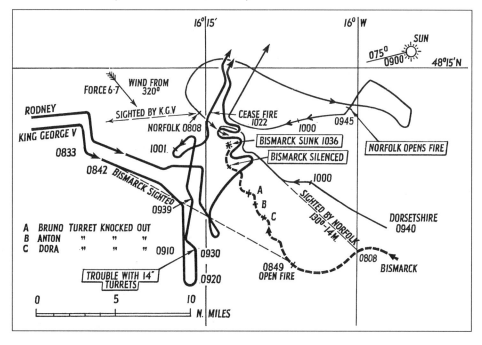

Index

—⁓—

2/12